Praise for *YOUR EFT BUSIN*
Creating Your Dream Practice

This isn't just a manual on how to become an EFT practitioner, but more a book that shows you how you can keep falling in love over and over again with what you do. It's certainly a book I will recommend to all the practitioners I train in the future and it will change the way EFT practitioners show up in their work for years to come.

Karl Dawson
EFT Master and Creator of Matrix Reimprinting

This book helps you recognise the value of YOU as an EFT practitioner. I was immediately drawn in by the style and impressive practical exercises that empower you to connect to your life purpose and create a business and life you love. This book is heartfelt, easy to read and full of accounts to inspire you. I've learnt a lot from reading it. Thank you Susie!

Kate Marillat
Co-author of *Transform Your Beliefs, Transform Your Life*

This book will empower you, in a step-by-step approach, to fully live your purpose, and to embrace all the aspects of your own tapping business.
As Susie says in the book, "There is a huge gap between what you perceive will happen and what actually takes place when building your business," and as you read, you will discover how to avoid common blocks that cause overwhelm, insecurity and "living in the gap between the vision you have for your business and the outcome in the real world".

Best of all, Susie will help you realise that you are not alone and that there is a solution.

Gary Williams
Director and CEO TappingHub.tv

There is little or nothing new about the ideas presented in this book, but its outstanding worth is that all these valuable ideas are drawn together and presented beautifully in one place. It is a book I would strongly recommend to everyone.

Its format is well thought-out and presented in a way that is both easy to read and informative. The presentation includes instruction and exercises, together with "Reflection Points" which lead the reader to reflect upon their reading and ideas in ways that they may never have thought about. The questions Susie asks draw you to look at matters in a way you may never have considered at all—they are quite eye-opening.

It is based on EFT, but it will not only be helpful to EFT therapists. Rather it is applicable to any branch of therapy, and, in fact, any branch of endeavour. I will certainly be recommending it to all my students (and to myself!).

Dr Tam Llewellyn-Edwards, PhD
Founder EFT Master and Therapy Trainer, UK

As soon as I began reading Susie's book, I knew that I would have loved having this for myself in 1980 when I first started my private practice.

Susie has covered all aspects needed to prepare and support you in creating a dream business, whatever therapy you may be using. Her own experience in her business and her skills in helping others mean that this is a must-have if you really want to get started or to feel inspired wherever you are in your therapy business journey.

This book knows exactly how to meet your emotional as well as your practical needs: it is going to become very dog-eared as well as loved. It will be there right beside you, opening your eyes to see the special gifts that you bring to your clients' lives. Even after thirty-five years in my therapy business, Susie's book reawakened me to more of my business potential. Only read this book if you want to reignite your passion for living on purpose. Thank you Susie for sharing your heartfelt wisdom so openly.

Mary Llewellyn
Founding EFT Master and Energy Therapy Trainer, UK

This book is not just for EFT practitioners, but a wonderful foundation book for anybody who would like to build a successful business and, more importantly, create the life of their dreams. It is packed full of exercises to help you transform your blocks to success and practical advice on how to build and market your business. *Your EFT Business* empowers you to clear your past, live more joyfully in the present and manifest from the future. How does it get any better than that!

Sharon King
Author of *Heal Your Birth, Heal Your Life: Tools to Transform Your Birth Experience and Create a Magical New Beginning*

For a number of years I trained EFT and Matrix Reimprinting practitioners around the world. I trained some of the brightest, shiniest and most talented people imaginable—people who were highly skilled at helping others to overcome their traumas and challenges. One of the things that I noticed consistently was that only a small handful of those made it as practitioners. Many just didn't have the business knowledge or skills to get their business off the ground. Others stood in their own way and didn't know how to move beyond their own blocks and challenges. This is the book I wished I had had for them all back then. It's an absolute gem of a resource and a reflection of Susie Shelmerdine's knowledge level in this area. Because of this book, a multitude of EFT practitioners are going to succeed in business where they didn't before. I am looking forward to the transformation this is going to create in the world. If you are considering buying this book to develop and improve your EFT business, it will undoubtedly be the best investment you make.

Sasha Allenby
Co-author of *Matrix Reimprinting Using EFT*, author of *Write an Evolutionary Self-Help Book* and CEO of Wisdompreneurs Publishing

Your EFT Business

The Essential Guide to Creating Your Dream Practice

by

Susie Shelmerdine

Disclaimer: This book is presented solely for educational purposes. The author is not offering it as legal, accounting, or other professional services advice. While best efforts have been used in preparing this book, the author makes no representations or warranties of any kind, and assumes no liabilities of any kind, with respect to the accuracy or completeness of the contents, and specifically disclaims any implied warranties of merchantability or fitness of use for a particular purpose. The author shall not be held liable or responsible to any person or entity with respect to any loss or incidental or consequential damages caused, or alleged to have been caused, directly or indirectly, by the information or programmes contained herein.

Your EFT Business: The Essential Guide to Creating Your Dream Practice **by Susie Shelmerdine**

ISBN: 978-0-9934091-0-3

Your EFT Business: The Essential Guide to Creating Your Dream Practice

Publisher: Sun, Moon and Star Publishing.

Contents

Foreword

Karl Dawson, EFT Master

Over the years I've trained literally thousands of practitioners in EFT and Matrix Reimprinting (an advanced tapping tool that I created myself). A large number of those whom I trained have gone on to become very successful practitioners. I'm proud to see them out in the world making a difference with this vital work.

Quite often I'll see people pass through the training and I'll get a really strong sense that they could become a phenomenal practitioner. I'll watch them doing sessions on the training as they fall in love with EFT, and I'll picture them going home and getting their practice off the ground. While many of them do, there are a large number who also slip through the net. Nine times out of ten, it's because they don't have the business knowledge required to create a successful practice. Their initial fire is put out when they take their passion into the real world and are hit with a barrage of things that they don't know how to do.

If you are new to starting or developing your practice, this book offers a whole host of practical solutions, which will take you step by step through the process of creating a thriving business. What I like most about this book is that it handles the practical side of setting up business, plus the emotional and energetic side.

We are confronted with many of our unresolved issues when we go into business. In my latest book, *Transform Your Beliefs, Transform Your Life*, I share how unresolved beliefs impact every aspect of your life, and this definitely includes business. If you don't transform those beliefs at a core level, they will impact your business on *every* level. I've seen time and time again what happens if people try to start a business without tackling these beliefs. But fortunately, I've also seen many examples of what happens when people do.

Because tools like EFT and Matrix Reimprinting are so powerful and effective, I've watched many of the people that I have trained applying them to their lives to create a highly successful business. There were people such as Erika Brodnock, who came on my training course when she was financially destitute and has since become the founder and CEO of Karisma Kidz, teaching children worldwide to be confident and happy. I have countless other stories of people who have transformed their lives with these tools and then gone on to help others do the same. Susie Shelmerdine was one of those success stories too.

When I first met Susie she practically crawled into my treatment room. She arrived as one of the many clients I was treating for chronic fatigue in those days. She also arrived as one of EFT's sceptics.

Despite her initial resistance, Susie had a hunger to heal that eventually paid off. She worked extensively on herself with EFT and Matrix Reimprinting. She had such a remarkable recovery that she was one of the first people to get EFT featured on TV in the UK. It was a proud moment for me when she appeared on BBC news.

Like many of the clients I have worked with, Susie became a practitioner and was eager to share her healing journey with others. She qualified in a diagnostic tool called Meta-Medicine, which helps identify the underlying emotional cause of a physical condition, and she soon advanced up the ranks to Meta-Medicine trainer. She trained others to use these tools alongside EFT and Matrix Reimprinting.

Although she was highly skilled at using these tools and always got great results, I often thought she would carve out something that was more uniquely her own. Frequently, when people overcome a health condition they become duty-bound to help others do the same. I've seen it in the many practitioners I have trained where they start out doing what they think they should be doing, and then evolve into their real purpose. When Susie began to use these tools to realise her own dreams and then help others do the same, it was obvious that she had found her calling.

What this book offers goes way beyond the mechanical process of how to become a successful EFT practitioner. It offers practitioners a way to discover what it is they are truly being called to do, beyond the initial honeymoon with EFT. Because Susie has found the courage to follow her true path with this work, she is in the ideal position to help others do the same. This isn't just a manual on how to become an EFT practitioner, but more a book that shows you how you can keep falling in love over and over again with what you do. It's certainly a book I will recommend to all the practitioners I train in the future and it will change the way EFT practitioners show up in their work for years to come.

EFT Master Karl Dawson – Creator of Matrix Reimprinting. Co-author of *Matrix Reimprinting Using EFT* and *Transform Your Beliefs, Transform Your Life*

Introduction

Do you remember the moment you first discovered EFT?

Whether you watched it in a demo or experienced it live, it was probably a moment that changed your life forever. For most of us, it was a turning point where reality flipped 180 degrees sideways and was never the same again. Up until that point you probably believed that emotions were something that happen to us and not something we have any control over. Yet right in front of you was a tool that could be easily learnt and self-applied, and could transform even the most complex of emotional triggers.

If not right away, then certainly somewhere along the line, it seems that you heard a calling. You literally *had* to share this with the world. You had to help others experience the same kind of freedom it was giving you. Maybe you started out tapping on those around you (and for some of us, it might have seemed like we tapped on everything with a pulse!), and as you saw results and lives started to change, it dawned upon you that this is what you were meant to do for a living. *This* was your calling. Undoubtedly the fire in your heart became so strong that there was literally no other choice. You had to make a difference with this tool. What else could you do?

If you have already started your business, then it is likely that you tentatively set up practice. If you were new to having clients, it probably felt like a minefield at first, but your enthusiasm carried you through. Yet perhaps, like most people in your position, there was a huge gap between what you perceived would happen and what actually took place. Maybe you created your flyers, scattering them around, and sat by the phone waiting for clients to call. As the days wore on and you didn't get the response you were looking for, you may have found yourself starting to think you had done something wrong. Suddenly, you found old issues of insecurity and self-doubt setting in. "Why is nobody coming? Is it me?" Questions like this started to run through your mind. Before you knew it, your enthusiasm was replaced by fear, overwhelm and insecurity, and once the doubt set in, you felt paralysed to move forward. Maybe you got the odd client here or there but it was nothing like you expected, and you found yourself living in the gap between the vision you had for your business and the outcome in the real world.

If this goes anywhere near to describing your journey, then you are definitely not alone. I've coached EFT practitioners from all over the world who have felt like they have somehow failed because their business didn't yield the results that they had visualised. And, in working with them, I've helped them create a business that had much more in common with their original vision after they worked with me.

Putting Yourself Out There

As EFT practitioners we want to change lives. The things that we have to do to put ourselves out there in order to impact those lives can feel like a distraction from our main purpose.

A small few rise to the challenge and embrace all the different components needed to enable a business to thrive. But the majority of us pull back, sometimes resisting and other times, downright refusing to put these pieces in place. Not only do we suffer, feeling frustration and that we aren't fulfilling our purpose, but we also have a nagging sense that we could be helping more people if these obstacles were removed. The result is a lose-lose situation. And subsequently we either become jaded or give up altogether.

Changing the Pattern

I wrote this book to help you change that pattern. I wrote it to empower you to have a completely different approach to building and creating your business. I wrote it because I want to inspire you to become more confident with building your message for your business and sharing it with your clients or your new customers. This book will empower you, step by step, to fully live your purpose, and to embrace all the aspects of your business. It will help you bridge the gap between the fantasy you had about working with clients and the reality of an ever-expanding client base. It will help you have more comfort and ease with everything from sending emails to prospective clients, to building your 'About Me' page on your website, to describing your work to a stranger, to setting your rates and charging what you are worth. As you work through this book, you will increase your confidence in 'unleashing yourself onto the world' — a confidence that will underpin everything that you do.

But before we dive into the nuts and bolts about how to create the business you've been dreaming about, I'd like to share a bit of my own background that led me to coaching individuals, just like you, to have a more thriving EFT practice.

Susie's Story – Creating a Thriving Practice

Like many people's journey with EFT, mine started when I was overcoming a debilitating health condition. A disabling experience with chronic fatigue syndrome left me unable to function in 2005, and I was forced to slow down and re-examine every aspect of my life and reality. Luckily I had found the tool in EFT that would help me do just that.

I first experienced it through EFT Master Karl Dawson, arriving as one of EFT's sceptics and being quickly won over by its effects. My healing was dramatic — so much so that I was featured on the BBC news in the UK, being one of the first to get EFT into the news in my country. Naturally I was hungry to share what I knew with the world.

But despite my enthusiasm for my new-found healing, I had a new challenge to overcome. Up until that point in my life, all I had known was trauma, drama and stress. It wasn't that I'd never created a successful business before. Prior to being sick I had an entertainment company and had previously worked in the corporate world, but success had come with a price. I'd work eighty long, hard, gruelling hours a week. So, I knew how to create a business but I didn't know how to do it joyfully. Work had always been self-punishing to me. Even as a child, the gruelling regime of ballet school lessons, professional performances and dance competitions meant that I never really knew how to just hang free and allow something to unfold.

I brought this old energy into my new business. It may not surprise you to learn that it didn't work. I pushed, I strove, I forced, and I soon found myself exhausted trying to promote the very technique that I'd healed myself with. There was obviously more work to do. But on a deeper level, there was also a sense that there had to be a better way. Just because I had been entrained with behaving this way towards my livelihood didn't mean it was the only way. I dedicated myself to finding a way to create a business model that was fun, light and easy to engage with. If I couldn't find it, I was going to create it. It was just that at first, I didn't know how.

My first turning point came from an unexpected source. I'd had a lifelong travel dream of going to the Caribbean. It had always seemed like one of those dreams that was way out of my reach. Yet I managed to save enough money to make it possible to go. As I stepped off the plane from the 11.5-hour flight, something struck me. It wasn't the wonder of actually making it or that feeling of "You did it Susie," that hit me, but another thought. The thought was "Well, that actually wasn't that hard to do, was it?" I wasn't undermining my efforts, but I realised I had built it up in my mind to be much further beyond my reach than it actually was, and in doing so I had created a gap between what I wanted to achieve and what I was creating in my life. Of course, I'd heard Law of Attraction teachers talk about this very phenomenon many times, but it wasn't until that point that I actually got it on a cellular level.

In that moment, five months after my recovery, I got the first glimpse of the fact that achieving my dreams could feel really natural to me. Of course, it is totally natural for us to have desires and expand into them. We just get in our own way, time and time again, with our patterns and our beliefs about how things are supposed to be.

It took, however, a few years for this realisation to really sink into my bones. It was only later when I went to live in Turkey, initially for a short period, that I realised this on a much deeper level. In that period I started writing a book on health. Although I had a lot of knowledge and information on the subject, it wasn't my passion and I was swimming upstream trying to write it. At that point, I took myself through the very things that are in this book. I began living from my passion rather than from a preconceived idea of who I thought I should be. And as soon as I committed to living that way, my dreams started to come true and I began to live the life that was more aligned with my true calling: travelling and empowering people to realise their own dreams.

I understood I'd been trying to create my business through struggle instead of joy. And the universe had been reflecting back to me the struggle that I had been feeling inside. What if I put my joy at the forefront of my business instead? What if I envisaged and created the life I wanted and built my business around that, instead of the reverse? I decided to put this question into action in my life.

Since then I have travelled and worked in England, Europe, Australia and America. I have seen kangaroos, koalas, lions, tigers and bears! I've visited the Golden Gate Bridge, the Empire State Building, and even manifested my childhood dream of meeting a cheetah. I relocated to Turkey and bought my dream apartment by the beach. But best of all, I have assisted people like yourself to find their zest for life and put it at the heart of their business. I've watched with amazement as they too have realised their dreams and helped transform lives at the same time.

I still have challenges like everyone else and am not immune to life's ups and downs. But I am living life from my heart, inspired by how much this work has impacted the clients I have worked with. And I'm passionate about sharing it with you so that you can experience similar results.

Our Journey Together

The information and exercises in this book are broadly divided into two themes. There is the intrinsic work that you need to do on yourself to prepare yourself for having a thriving business. Then there is the extrinsic work that you need to do in your business and the wider world in order to make yourself known to your potential client base.

Most of us don't prepare ourselves for being in business, so we will begin there, looking at your motivation for starting a business and who you are in your business. We'll look at your relationship to your business, enabling you to establish a healthy bond so that you can move forward synergistically. We'll also examine and transform any underlying beliefs or fears that you have about being out in the world.

Once we've looked at you and helped you transform any beliefs that might be holding you back, we will turn our attention to your message. We'll help you shape a unique message, exploring the option of specialising in a particular field or being more of a general practitioner. Once you know what your unique message is, we'll help you take it out into the world, supporting you to develop your presence, effectively market your business, and attract clients.

Next we'll explore your relationship with money, checking you aren't carrying any old beliefs or programmes that are preventing you from manifesting more.

Finally, we'll help you to create a plan and stay motivated, so that you don't give up on the challenging days, and so that you keep sight of the big picture while celebrating each smaller success.

Whether you are just starting out or have been running your practice for some time, the tools and processes contained in this book will enable you to become more business savvy, which will ultimately support you in realising your dream of becoming a successful EFT practitioner and helping countless others to create changes in their lives.

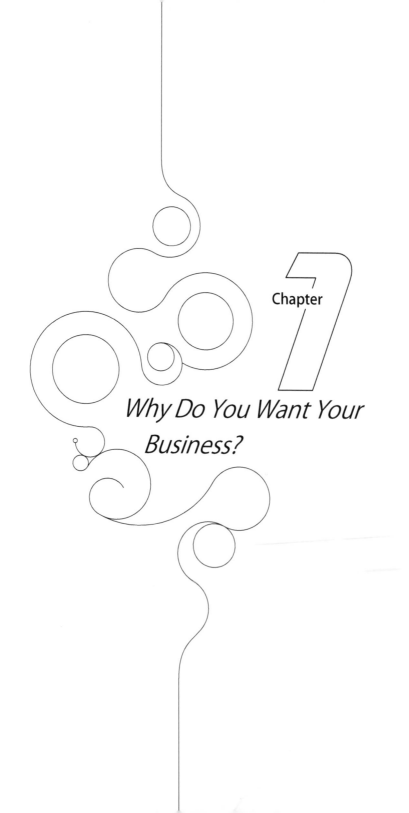

Chapter

_1_

Why Do You Want Your Business?

Your journey into business starts with you. While you may be led by selfless motivations such as changing lives or making a huge impact on others, it is vital to start with you, or more specifically, what you want out of your business. Yet most of us don't start there. The majority of us have a vision to set up a practice without actually sitting down and addressing our 'big why'. Not the shallow, superficial why, but the deep underlying why that sits at the centre of all that we do.

Your big why comes from beyond your persona of yourself as a therapist, or anywhere you may have defined yourself in a certain role. It also comes from beyond other people's perceptions or expectations of you. Your big why comes from deep within you. Yet if you don't face it and address it, your business can resemble a ship without a rudder. Because your big why is the heartbeat that keeps your business alive and motivates you on the days where you might otherwise give up or lose faith in what it is you do. And your big why *has* to be fuelled by why you want your business in the first place. It has to be more than what you can give your business. It has to centre around what your business can give you.

BUSINESS FOUNDATION

Like anything else in life you need a good foundation for your business. Just as when a house is being built it relies on a good foundation, the same can be said of your business. The foundation for your business starts with knowing why you actually *want* your business. There are other foundational pieces such as having a clear message based on knowing what your clients' needs are, and we will explore these later in this book. But first and foremost, we want to build your business based on why you want it.

Many of us start to try and manifest clients or grow a new business without defining this, and the results are not usually the ones we desired. When you've answered why you want your business, you are more confident in your services and marketing. Because they are based on a deep inner knowing of what you want your business to bring you, you are more in rapport with what you are doing, checking in frequently to see where you are with it, expanding, developing and growing it. It becomes a dynamic relationship rather than something that is static.

WHAT'S IN IT FOR YOU?

When I coach emerging business leaders, particularly those who have just started out, one of the first questions that I ask is "What's in it for you?" This question can trigger a lot of discomfort at first, and you may be having a similar experience yourself as you read these words. Quite often I am met with an answer such as "I want to be in service," or "I'm not interested in my own gains." In truth, when I hear answers such as these I know that, while the intentions are good, they are actually misguided, and there are going to be challenges in the business as a result.

There has been a fashion in the self-help and transformation industry to give answers like those above. It comes from a misguided notion that we are meant to be self-sacrificing in our service to others. Although this is a noble idea, it does not offer a practical approach to being in business in the West. In many Eastern cultures, sages and spiritual teachers aren't paid. Alternatively, they are supported by their followers and are provided food, clothing and shelter. This dynamic has marked the way we do therapeutic business in the West, leaving many people with the notion that we should not charge for what we do, and that it should be a form of self-sacrifice. However, Western culture operates under a different system. Our therapeutic practices *are* a business, and unless we treat them as such, then we will limit ourselves to doing the occasional session with family and friends, or giving our time for free — at the expense of our livelihood.

YOUR LIFE PURPOSE

Beyond the practicalities of putting a roof over our heads and food on our tables, there is a much broader picture of what motivates us in business. When we talk about our practice as a means to pay our bills, we are focusing on it as a means to survive. If you see your practice purely as a means for survival, it will not thrive either. You will start to see each client as a food ticket and they will get a sense of your desperation, particularly if you are not operating so successfully. You will take on clients that, in your heart, you know you aren't best suited to helping so that you can make the money you need to live. This is what generally occurs when we build a practice purely on survival needs and not on our life purpose.

So, your life purpose isn't just to pay the bills. It is also creatively contributing in a way that makes you feel good. It is how you express the passion of the highest version of yourself. It is either what you came here to do or what you are being called to do in this period of your life. If you haven't pinpointed it already, in Chapter 2 we are going to enable you to get really clear on what that purpose is and how you can uniquely express it. For now, it needs to be part of the equation of why you want your business.

But your big why needs to contain an even deeper component beyond doing what you came here to do. Because if you get lost in your quest for your 'life purpose', it can be easy to just think of it as something that is extrinsic to you. In other words, when we talk about purpose, it can be easy to interpret that as "What am I useful for?" If we aren't careful, that can take us right back to where we started and we can find ourselves serving others without really asking what we truly want.

There is also an intrinsic purpose that fires what we do. Our intrinsic purpose for our business is the fulfilment of the goals and dreams that we want to achieve in life outside of our work or career. I'm not talking about the accumulation of material wealth, but more specifically about your deep desires for your external reality: acquiring goods, the meditation retreat you've wanted to go on, the place you've always wanted to relocate to, the personal development retreat that you have longed to go on every year since you saw it advertised, or that dream of creating a life of travelling to far-flung locations more often than you do now.

The bottom line is, if your business is thriving you can fund your goals and dreams. And one of the core messages of this book is that it is perfectly natural to have these desires and want your business to fund them. It is part of your life purpose to have experiences you desire. However, what tends to happen is we feel ashamed of thinking of ourselves in this way, as many of us are still operating under the old paradigm belief that it isn't OK to profit from being in service to others. It causes us to live divided, claiming on the surface that we are just in it to help others, yet secretly finding ourselves harbouring the desire for a better life or feeling guilty when we celebrate life with the money we earned from a client.

I believe this cycle is why a number of practitioners subconsciously keep their business just at the rate at which they can survive (and for many, it is below that rate). When we break this pattern, we can unite our dedication to helping others with our life purpose, fuelling these by living the life that we love. When we do this, we do not separate our passion from our service to others. Instead, our passion *fuels* our service to others. We then become a much more valuable role model to our clients, because we are valuing ourselves accordingly. We start to truly live our purpose.

EVERYTHING IS AN EXCHANGE

So, to reiterate, as soon as you separate your deepest desires in life from your business, it becomes mechanical and dead. But if your business is fuelled by your passion and purpose, then you breathe life into that which you love, and the two in turn fire each other.

Everything is an exchange, and what you are giving out you need to be able to receive in return. It is a two-way process.

Recently when he spoke in New York, the Dalai Lama echoed similar sentiments. He talked of how giving to yourself and giving to others aren't separate, but are one and the same. Yet many people are surprised when they hear someone like the Dalai Lama say things like this. The stereotype of one in service leaves them to assume that service only goes outwards. However, spiritual leaders such as the Dalai Lama understand that it also goes inwards, and the amount you are prepared to give yourself is reflected in the amount you can show up for others, and vice versa.

If you understand this fundamental principle, your whole relationship with yourself and your business will change radically. Up until now, you may have perceived being in service to others as something self-sacrificing. The irony is that, if you are operating under this paradigm, not only are you doing yourself a disservice, but your clients too. A number of your clients may be coming to you with issues of scarcity. Others might be coming to you because they don't know how to value themselves or put themselves first. But if you have a self-sacrificing notion about being in service to them, you are not modelling abundance or extreme self-care. You will not truly be able to help them overcome these, or similar issues, if you are still operating from a paradigm of self-sacrificing and not filling your own cup.

REFLECTION POINT:

What's your business going to provide in your life? If you have dreams and goals, what are they? This is what your business is going to be funding, so you need to get creative.

Notice if you have separated your fun, joy and dreams from your business. If you have compartmentalised them, it is probably due to a Western work ethic, which teaches us that our work is something to be laboured at. From this perspective, we treat our business as a workhorse that needs to be tended to. Reflect how much you have been operating under this paradigm and then ask yourself what it is you want from your business beyond this old model. Notice how your energy around your business changes when you shift your paradigm around it.

Tap for any beliefs such as "Nothing good comes without hard work," "Success doesn't come easily," "No pain, no gain," "There is no room for emotion in business," etc., that keep you held in the old paradigm.

DIARY PLANNING

The model that I present in this book is to create a life plan *first* and then to fit your business into that life plan. Sometimes when I've suggested to clients that they plan their life first, I have heard them answer, "Planning my life is not bringing in clients." If you are operating from a scarcity model, you will believe it is a waste of time to do anything other than the activities that are going to build the business, particularly if you aren't making any money. There can be a tendency to feel guilty when we aren't doing things that contribute to the business, which means we never end up having fun because our time out is always marred by a sense that we should be doing something to bring in clients. However, when your energy is really secure in what you are doing and why you're doing it, the universe responds in a very different way. For example, if you decide that you only work with clients between 10 and 3 so you can give the most focused attention to your children when they come home from school, you are more likely to attract clients who want a session in this time, or who are willing to alter their own schedules so that they can work with you in this time. Similarly, if you know you function much better if you meditate and eat breakfast before your sessions, and you incorporate this into your day, you are less likely to skip the things that work for you.

Living in Turkey, I ensure that I prioritise my swim with the turtles, allowing a couple of hours every day to do that. If I booked sessions in this time I know I would feel divided or even resentful. I ensure I take this precious time and it means that during my sessions I am able to show up more present for my clients. As soon as I got clear on this, I opened up some evening sessions, and almost immediately I had clients contacting me and asking me if I was available in the evenings. It all has very much to do with your resonance of what you are doing and how you are relating that to the rest of your life.

One of my clients on my webinar programme for practitioners had a similar experience. She blocked time out for her son and ensured that she took no clients at that time. When she had become very specific about this, she described how she no longer felt she was forcing her business onto her life, but rather creating a relationship with her business and her life together. When you do this, you don't feel guilty about telling a client that you don't work during that time. You've moved out of the purely service model where you feel you should be there for your clients morning, noon and night, and into a model where you decide when you are in service and when you are engaging with other aspects of your life. At this point, your business becomes a part of what you do, and is not central to who you are.

FUTURE DIARY EXERCISE:

This exercise was inspired by one of our course members on the *Realise Your Magical Business* programme that I delivered with Sharon King.

It is vital when creating your business that you examine the actual time you have for it. We all tend to think we have more time for our business than we do.

I suggest you carry out this exercise for a minimum of one month, and anywhere up to a year. This exercise usually works best when you purchase a diary that is especially for this exercise, particularly one that you find is elegant or that generates positive emotion.

Start by flicking through your old diary. Notice if it is empty in places. If this generates strong emotions, tap on them to bring them down before you start creating your future diary; consider any underlying beliefs that may need addressing too. For example, if you have lots of gaps in your diary, you might be hearing an accompanying voice that says, "I've failed."

Now take your future diary and start to schedule how you would like your life to be. Start by scheduling in the free time and holidays that you would like to have. It may be the weekends or free time in the week. Block them out in a colour that represents holidays to you.

Next go through the diary and schedule in your time with family and friends. Perhaps there are regular events you want to attend with them each week and there may be more specific, one-off events that you would like to spend time on. Choose a colour for family and friends and block these events out too.

Now schedule in fun and enjoyable activities. These might include workshops, yoga classes, walking the dog, the hairdresser's, having a massage, reading or bath time. Use a separate colour for your enjoyable activities.

Now add anything that you regularly have to do, like taking the kids to school, cooking, cleaning, and so on. Add your regular tasks in a different colour.

Next, choose the amount of hours each week that you would like to work with clients. You may even schedule in trainings and talks if this is something you are either doing or wish to expand into. Ensure that you don't fill all the remaining time with working with clients, because you'll need to leave time for marketing, promoting, blogging, accounting, creating and learning new skills— otherwise your business will become stagnant.

For some people it works to spend three days a week working with clients and one day for marketing, admin and business growth. Alternatively, you might spread your administrative and development tasks throughout the week.

Flick back through your new diary and check in with yourself. How does it feel with your diary filling up in this way? Does it feel joyful? If not, what are the beliefs or messages that you are hearing as you flip through the future diary? Perhaps there is doubt or overwhelm. Whatever you feel, tap on it, until the only feeling remaining about your future diary is one of excitement.

'Sarah's' Results

When 'Sarah' carried out this exercise on one of my webinars, she established that she had space for six clients a week at ninety minutes each. She already had a part-time job and any more clients would take her away from her family commitments.

She also realised she might need to bring in extra childcare as she was always rushing to do the 2 pm school run.

This exercise often enables practitioners to realise when they need to delegate in order to be more productive.

WHAT'S RIGHT FOR YOU?

Often when we set up a business we think we have to be back-to-back with clients. As a successful practitioner of these tools for a number of years, I used to run myself into the ground with clients. Now I don't see any more than ten clients a week, by choice. In honesty, when I work with more than ten clients I start to feel a little overwhelmed, especially as I always take time to review my notes and creatively think about how I can help my clients with their challenges outside the session. For a three-month period I was seeing twelve to sixteen clients a week on top of my promotion and marketing, and I started to burn out. My relationships were affected, I was snapping at people, and I didn't have the capacity to help my friends and relatives outside of the sessions when they had challenges. These are the kinds of things that give when we spread ourselves too thinly.

So it is vital to look at where your capabilities are, especially if you are seeing lots of clients with big-T traumas and serious health conditions. As an EFT practitioner, you might be going from a session about a car crash, to one about child abuse, to one about a natural disaster, to one about a phobia, to one about an addiction. Even though you are tapping with your clients the whole time and supporting them to create massive changes in their lives, you are still human, and you need to be able to have time to take yourself out of the energy field of trauma in order to feel centred and whole again. If you don't, you will likely burn out.

Summary of Chapter One

a. **The foundation for your business starts with knowing why you actually** *want* **your business.** The majority of us have a vision to set up a practice without actually sitting down and addressing our 'big why'. Your big why is the heartbeat that keeps your business alive and motivates you on the days where you might otherwise give up or lose faith in what it is you do. It is essential to fuel your big why with the reason you want your business in the first place.

b. **In setting up business it is essential to ask, "What's in it for me?"** Many of us have been misguided by the notion that we should only be in service. Yet part of being in service is giving equally back to yourself what you give out to others. You need to ensure that your business is giving to you and not just taking from you.

c. **It is essential to align your business with your life purpose.** Your life purpose isn't just to pay the bills. It is also creatively contributing in a way that makes you feel good. It is how you express the passion of the highest version of yourself. This needs to be part of the equation of why you want your business.

d. **If your business is thriving, you can fund your goals and dreams.** The old paradigm belief is that it isn't OK to profit from being in the service of others. It causes us to live divided, claiming on the surface that we are just in it to help others, yet secretly finding ourselves harbouring the desire for a better life or feeling guilty when we celebrate life with the money we earned from a client. The new paradigm is a balance of both in a model of exchange.

e. **Ask yourself what's right for you.** Often when we set up a business we think we have to be back-to-back with clients. Instead, it is vital to look at where your capabilities and other commitments are and to plan mindfully so you don't burn out.

Chapter

2

Who Are You in Your Business?

What's your unique selling point?

It's a question that can make many of us feel uncomfortable. For the most part, it makes us look at our business, and question whether what we have created is anything special or new. Often when we are asked this question, we compare ourselves to others, looking at what we have created with our insecurities triggered to the maximum. "Perhaps I should just give up, as I have nothing special to offer," we conclude, when we determine that we haven't created anything new.

If this scenario is a familiar one, or if you have been avoiding the question of whether you actually have a unique selling point (USP), then this chapter will help you move beyond those challenges. Because your unique selling point is actually *you*.

In the last chapter we asked you to look deeply at why you want your business, and in this chapter we are going to look at who you are in business. Not your persona of who you are, based on a collection of things you have learnt about yourself in your life up until now, but the true, authentic you.

THE ROLE OF YOU IN BUSINESS

Many of us show up in business in a role. It is usually based upon a collection of assumptions that we have about what it means to *be* in business. The role that we create for ourselves will be based upon our conditioning and programming, along with our life experiences. As an EFT practitioner, you already understand how your past experiences shape who you are today, but have you really stopped to examine how they shape who you are in business? Yet your perception of yourself in business will be fundamental to how others perceive you and whether they choose to invest in you.

EVERYBODY HAS A GIFT

EFT is not what you do. It is a tool. It is not your uniqueness. Instead, you are your own uniqueness.

Whatever tool you are practicing, whether it has changed your life or the lives of those around you, isn't who you are. It is you who are using the tool. You are bringing your own life experience of how to apply these tools to the issues that your clients bring to you. But the key to your business is not the tools. The key is you.

If you think the tools alone are what create the change, then you are missing a vital component of this work. You are placing all the power and the magic in the tools. Yes, they are magnificent. But a big part of that magnificence comes from you and what you do with them.

When you ask people what they are looking for in a practitioner, it isn't usually the tools they are looking for. People buy people — they don't buy a tool or technique. When you understand this and can confidently stand by you, rather than hiding behind your tools, your whole business will evolve significantly.

> **REFLECTION POINT:**
>
> What is your uniqueness?
> What do your clients gain from you?

When you know your uniqueness, it helps you to stop comparing yourself to others or perceiving people who do something similar to you as competition.

At one point, a friend invited me to a business meeting. I didn't actually want to go, so I didn't pay much attention to what it was about. Eventually I let her talk me into it. When I turned up, everybody was dressed very formally and I realised it wasn't the small event that I thought it would be. It was actually a very prestigious event with over four hundred people in attendance. I had dressed casually, and was wearing a flowery sundress and a denim jacket with my hair scraped back. It was one of those awkward moments where you realise you haven't dressed for the occasion.

I made a vital decision in those opening moments: "I am just going to be me." For the rest of the evening I was authentically myself in every conversation. I soon found myself surrounded by people who wanted to talk to me, and those who weren't resonating with what I had to say quickly moved on.

At one moment I walked up to a renowned businessman. He asked me, "What do you do?" and I replied, "I inspire and empower people worldwide to realise their dreams and live a life of their choice. And I want an interview for my book. Are you in?" He replied, "That sounds fabulous. I don't know what it is but I'm in."

I'd dropped the role of Susie and was just showing up as myself, and some of the connections I made during that evening are still thriving today. They came from me, operating from my unique gift and not from any preconceived idea of who I thought I should be.

DEFINING YOUR PURPOSE

Everyone has been made for some particular work.
And the desire for that work has been put in every heart.

Rumi

As we touched upon in Chapter 1, your purpose is what you came here to do. When we talk about purpose, remember we are not just talking about your being in service. We are talking about the qualities you bring to this world and expressing them in a way that is unique to you.

When you are living on purpose the world feels like a completely different place. In many ways, living on purpose enables us to be more present. On the other hand, if we are ignoring our unique purpose, it often feels like there is something we have forgotten. It will keep eating away at us, causing us to live divided. In the first case, we are here in this moment, and in the second, there is a sensation or feeling — something that we can't quite put our finger on — that is nudging us towards our true north.

The reason we avoid this feeling is that often we are too caught up in our perception of what we think we should be doing, to carry out our actual calling. Our programming and conditioning create beliefs that feel stronger than our true calling. With these beliefs running the show, we buckle down to less rewarding work. We talk of duty or obligation or other concepts with a heavy energy. We let ourselves be weighed down by them and in turn, we move further and further away from what our heart wants us to achieve.

As we begin to heal our beliefs with EFT and other tools, we often start to see our true purpose emerging. For many people, it can mean that a lifetime's worth of work and studying needs to be put aside so that we can truly show up for what it is we are being called to do. I've seen this on countless occasions. One UK-based GP went to study EFT and Matrix Reimprinting with EFT Master Karl Dawson. She began to understand that she had chosen her particular career because she felt duty-bound to her parents and obligated to help others. As she healed her life experiences that had triggered her career decision, being a doctor was no longer appealing to her. She left the profession to work on her poetry!

In fact, more people make a career decision based on what happened to them as a child than you might think. The boy who was treated unjustly in life grows up to become a defence attorney. The girl who was not heard grows up to become a lecturer. Often when you heal the underlying beliefs that have led to the career choice, a different path emerges. You may be having a similar experience in your own life.

SEEING YOUR UNIQUE GIFTS

Have you noticed how other people might see unique gifts in you that you don't see in yourself? Perhaps you have heard people tell you that you are a great listener or that you are good at solving problems. It can be challenging to see our own unique gifts, as for most of us, they just feel like what we do naturally. Yet being able to recognise them, own them and utilise them is part of you defining your purpose.

When you know what your purpose is, it helps you define your message. And when you know what your message is, you can effectively communicate to your prospective clients about what you are able to offer them. In Chapter 6 we will explore your unique message and support you to create a message that reflects your purpose and your passion. First of all though, we need to define your purpose by recognising what your unique gifts are and shaping them into a business and brand that is unique to you. It will contain all the colours and textures of who you are and how you show up in the world. It will be a reflection of who you are in life, and we will build your business and brand on that, making it central to all that you do.

REFLECTION POINT:
WHAT ARE YOUR UNIQUE GIFTS?

This is not a time to be humble! Make a list of your unique gifts. Assuming you are still working towards a thriving EFT practice or improving the one that you have, start with your people skills. Are you intuitive? Do you listen carefully? Are you heart-centred or approachable?

Next move onto your wider skills. List your practical and other life skills.

Now connect with what you are passionate about. What sets your heart on fire? Is there a way to marry your people skills, your practical skills and your passion? You might not find the answer to this question straight away, but ask it as an open-ended question and see where you are drawn.

SPARKS AND FLAMES

When you have found your purpose, it will feel like it has a spark. You will stop operating mechanically and the spark within you will ignite a fire. This is crucial, because if your business doesn't ignite a spark in you, how is it going to ignite the spark in others? This might be the single most important question that anyone asks you in business. It isn't just about the initial spark, but how the fire keeps burning. In Chapter 4 you are going to learn how to be in relationship with your business, and this relationship is a dynamic interplay between your personal growth and expansion, and the development of your business, along with the fire for what you are doing.

As you grow, your purpose might change. Because you are someone who is prepared to face their blocks and dissolve them using the tools of EFT, you might be a completely different person tomorrow than you are today. The more you resolve your filters, beliefs and blocks about your identity and capability, the more you are likely to move fearlessly towards your true purpose.

My purpose has changed many times since I started out in this industry. It took me a while to arrive at helping people to realise their dreams. When I started out, I'd just healed a chronic health condition and gone from being disabled and bed-bound to complete health. Naturally I wanted to share what I had experienced with others. I let my recent experiences dictate my career choice and plunged into learning more about serious disease. I became highly skilled at using a diagnostic tool called Meta-Medicine, and developed a successful career supporting others who were on a journey of self-healing. I had some phenomenal experiences and appreciated every client that I worked with. But, as I said, the choice was based on my life experience of being sick, and not my true calling. My passion for helping others heal started to waver. It was a personal crisis at first as I wasn't sure what I was supposed to do. But as I relaxed into it, I realised that there was a similar, but more aligned, calling to help others achieve their dreams. If I'd remained attached to my original 'plan' or to the fact that I'd spent thousands of hours studying Meta-Medicine and gaining experience with clients in the field of health and disease, I would have been doing myself, and my clients, a disservice. Instead, I was willing to surrender what I had built to allow something that was even more unique to me to come through. I will continue to operate under the same model for the rest of the time I am in business, because I know too well what happens when we allow a choice we made some years ago to dictate what we do today, and when we don't allow ourselves to outgrow our choices. This happens in other areas of life, such as relationships. It is my belief that those who are truly happy in life are the ones who are willing to let go of yesterday's decisions if they don't serve them today, and I invite you to keep doing the same until you find what it is that you are truly here for.

CHOOSING TEN SECONDS AT A TIME

One way to help you ensure that you are opening up to surrendering to your purpose is to allow yourself to choose, ten seconds at a time. There is a tool called Access Consciousness, created by Gary Douglas, and one of its main principles is that a choice is only good for ten seconds. In other words, the person that you are in the next ten seconds, minutes, hours, days, weeks, months, years or decades, might require a different choice to the one you are making now. It gives you permission to grow out of your choices instead of using your previous choices to limit yourself.

If you have been using your previous choices to keep you locked into your current reality, it is only because this is what you have been entrained to do. In the West we are taught to choose a career at eighteen and pretty much stick with it. It is unlikely that you would listen to the career advice of an eighteen-year-old now. Yet for those of us who are still unhappily hanging on to a choice we made back then, that is exactly what we are doing.

REFLECTION POINT:

Have you ever had an experience of meeting someone that was on fire with their purpose? When you listened to them, you may not have even understood what they were talking about, but you felt the magical fire of their passion. Think of someone who fits this description. If you can't picture someone that you have met, go for a more obvious choice like Anthony Robbins. Regardless of whether you connect with his material or not, there is no disputing that he is in line with what he does. That's the kind of energy we are looking for. Now the question is, when do *you* feel like that? Have there been times in your life when you've noticed that your passion and your fire have gathered a crowd around you at a party or social event when you were speaking with love about what you do?

Follow up: Begin opening yourself up to this kind of fire. Don't judge yourself if it isn't there yet. But be willing to get out of your own way enough so it comes through (and remember you have a brilliant tool at your disposal if you keep getting in your own way!).

The reason that leading with your fire is so important is that you want your clients to be attracted to your flame. You want them to get into that zone with you. There is a reason they are seeking you out, and they are going to be drawn more by how you make them feel than what you actually say. When they buy into your enthusiasm in this way, you don't need to be as sharp at sales pitches or worry if you miss something out in your initial meeting. That first connection is going to be about what you transmit to them, and not about you being word-perfect. They are going to buy into your spark, and this is not something that can be faked. Your enthusiasm will show them a resonant match for what it is they are asking for, and their decision will be based on that, first and foremost. This kind of approach is a fast track to your client connection. It literally helps you zone into your clients and meet them with the sense that you are going to be able to help them overcome their challenges. And it goes without saying that you can only do this if you are being true to you.

'Jenny'

'Jenny' was a participant on one of our webinar programmes. She was terrified about going back to her old way of life. She'd qualified as a practitioner and had some success, but her business wasn't yielding the results she needed to stay in full-time practice. I worked with her, helping her to move out of presenting herself as an EFT practitioner, and instead tuning into her passion about who she was and why she loved to do this work with others. Her whole approach to sharing what she did changed. Just one week later, there was a message on the webinar forum. In Jenny's words: "I've got ten clients this week. Woo-hoo!!" Jenny is a classic example of what happens when we truly line up who we are with what we are doing. The universe responds accordingly to our passion, and the fire that we feel inside of ourselves is passed on to others too.

REALISE YOUR DREAMS

The following **Life Purpose Exercise** was taken from Jack Canfield's book *How to Get From Where You Are to Where You Want To Be*.

List two of your unique personal qualities, such as enthusiasm and creativity.

List one or two ways you enjoy expressing those qualities when interacting with others to support and inspire.

Assume the world is perfect right now. What would it look like? How is everyone interacting with everyone else? What does it feel like? Write your answer as a statement, in present tense, describing the ultimate condition, the perfect world as you see it and feel it. Remember: a perfect world is a fun place to be!!

Example: Everyone is freely expressing their own unique talents. Everyone is working in harmony. Everyone is expressing love.

Combine the three prior subdivisions of this exercise into a single statement.

Example: My purpose is to use my creativity and enthusiasm to support and inspire others to freely express their talent in a harmonious and loving way. Say your statement out loud. How does it feel to say it? How joyful does it make you feel? Rate your statement out of 10, 1 being that you feel bad about it and 10 being that it feels awesome. If it isn't a 10 out of 10 that sets your soul alight, then play with the wording. What changes could make it really resonate?

High on Life

Did you know that living your purpose may actually be good for your health?

During the years of working in the health industry, I noticed how a positive chemical reaction could reduce the negative impact of stress and trauma. When we are in stress, our hypothalamus-pituitary-adrenal access gets triggered and our adrenaline levels go up. The result is circulation of more cortisol in the body, which leaves us open to stress-related conditions.

Living our dreams means we are naturally in a state of heightened euphoria and subsequently, more high on life. And when we are high on life, we elevate the endogenous opioids, the body's versions of morphine and heroin. This is what gives you the feeling of the natural high because the body is producing higher levels of dopamine in the brain. If you have had that euphoric feeling after a session with a client, you will know what I mean. Our bodies also produce a hormone, oxytocin, and it plays a significant role in our cardiovascular system. It releases a chemical called nitrous oxide that reduces blood pressure and enables better oxygen circulation and heart function. So loving what you do is good for your health too!

Summary of Chapter Two

a. **Your unique selling point is *you*.** EFT is not what you do. It is a tool. It is not your uniqueness. Instead, you are your own uniqueness. If you think the tools alone are what create the change, then you are missing a vital component of this work.

b. **When you know your uniqueness, it helps you to stop comparing yourself to others**, or perceiving people who do something similar to you as competition.

c. **Your purpose is what you came here to do.** When we

talk about purpose, remember we are not just talking about your being in service. We are talking about the qualities you bring to this world and expressing them in a way that is unique to you.

d. **Our programming and conditioning create beliefs that feel stronger than our true calling.** With these beliefs running the show, we buckle down to less rewarding work. We let ourselves be weighed down by them and in turn, we move further and further away from what our heart wants us to achieve.

e. **When you know what your purpose is, it helps you define your message.** And when you know what your message is, you can effectively communicate to your prospective clients about what you are able to offer them.

f. **When you have found your purpose, it will feel like it has a spark.** You will stop operating mechanically and the spark within you will ignite a fire.

g. **As you grow, your purpose might change.** The more you resolve your filters, beliefs and blocks about your identity and capability, the more you are likely to move fearlessly towards your true purpose.

h. **Choose ten seconds at a time.** This Access Consciousness tool can help ensure that you are opening up to surrendering to your purpose. Allow yourself to choose ten seconds at a time. If you have been using your previous choices to keep you locked into your current reality, this tool will support you to make new choices that reflect who you are as you grow and evolve.

i. **Living your purpose may actually be good for your health.** Living your dreams means you are naturally in a state of heightened euphoria and are subsequently more high on life.

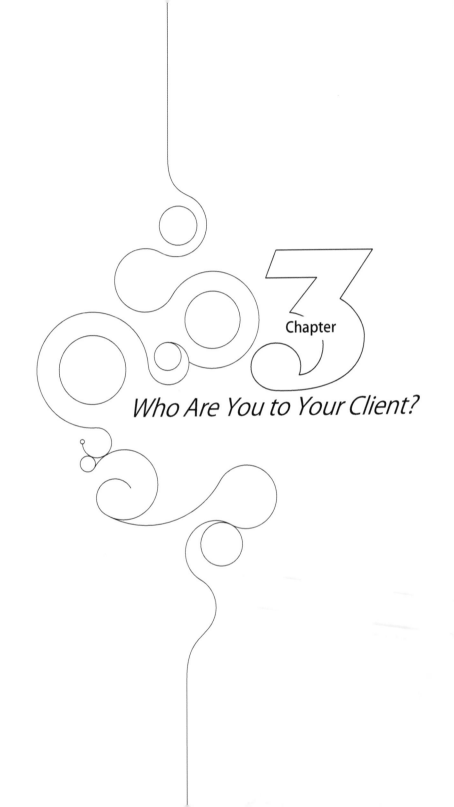

Chapter

3

Who Are You to Your Client?

Have you ever sat down and thought, "What is it that I actually offer my clients?"

It sounds like an obvious question, but when I ask it of the majority of clients that I coach, they are shocked to realise that they haven't really thought about the answer.

Something that I commonly hear is, "I'm offering them EFT," (or whatever their predominant modality is). But just as in the last chapter where we determined that you are not the tools that you practice, the tools are not actually what the client receives either. You might use the tools, but to define what your client receives by the tools you use is like building a house and defining it by the hammer and nails you used. The hammer and nails helped create the building, but they are not the building. The same can be said for the tools you practice.

When we look at the question of what you offer your clients on a deeper level, most of us are offering our clients the chance to profoundly change their lives. Your work is tremendously empowering. Even if you haven't started yet and haven't experienced the euphoria of seeing someone totally transform in front of you, it is likely that you have had a transformation in your own life using these tools, or seen someone else have the same, and that inspired you to become a practitioner. It is this potential to create change in someone's life that needs to sit at the heart of how you define yourself to your clients, and not the tools themselves.

LOOKING DEEPER AT YOU

When you ask why you are offering these services, the first place you need to look is you. What is it that *you* get from using these techniques with others? When you carry out a session, and you see that your clients have a shift, however large or small, what happens within you? Because if you aren't able to articulate the value of what it is you do, then how are your clients going to be able to connect with that same value? Part of this is about you owning what you do to the point where there is no doubt for your clients why they are drawn to working with you. You need to enable them to feel confident and secure in their work with you, and that has to start with you.

Are you the expert that they are coming to in order to gain specific knowledge? Are you a mentor that could help them on a journey of transformational change? Are you there to help them find a solution to a problem? Are you the source of inspiration or empowerment for them? Perhaps you are one of the few people in the world that they can trust or be honest with.

Getting clear on who you are for your clients isn't just for you. It's for them too. Because if you can confidently know what it is you are deeply offering, then it makes it much easier for your clients to receive it.

> **REFLECTION POINT:**
>
> Whether you are already in practice or have been doing swap sessions, look at some of the people who have come to you for help so far. Put yourself in their shoes. What are you offering them? What are they receiving from you?
>
> When you have picked a practitioner in the past, what specific qualities have you looked for? Can you recognise the same qualities in yourself, or do you have different ones to offer your clients?

When I was recovering from long-term illness, the practitioner I worked with was EFT Master Karl Dawson. Even though I was introduced to EFT by someone else, I searched for the right practitioner for me on the Internet, and came across Karl. It was obvious that he possessed the skill set that I was seeking. He had a background of working with my specific health condition. In addition, he had a presence that I instantly resonated with. I knew straight away that he was going to be my mentor and I was going to learn from him.

Despite this, I still turned up to our initial session with scepticism. I had my own beliefs and barriers to overcome. But the point is that Karl was solid enough in what he did to not be distracted by my defensive barriers. He held true to his inner belief in what he did, meeting me where I was, but moving me quickly on. He wouldn't have been able to achieve the same results with me if he hadn't been sure of himself, because he would have floundered at my scepticism.

Being Honest in the Sessions

As EFT practitioners, most of us offer a quality to our clients that is unique to the work that we do. We offer the opportunity for emotional honesty. We all know that EFT brings up emotions. Most of the time in an EFT session, your client can't hide their emotions from you. Crying on someone a few times usually breaks down the walls of the ego enough to go to a deeper level of connection, beyond the role or persona that your client may be used to displaying. However, they have to trust you enough in the first place to let the emotional barriers crumble.

Sometimes it can be quite overwhelming to consider who you are to your client. If you allow yourself to get in the way, it can feel like a daunting responsibility to be the gatekeeper of such intense emotional responses. As practitioners we have to monitor ourselves when it comes to the amount of emotions we are capable of evoking in people. On one end of the scale is our fear that we won't be able to handle what comes up or that it will trigger our own stuff. And on the other end, there is a danger of allowing our egos to take centre stage and for us to confuse the power of the transformation that the client experiences with who we are to our client. We need to find a middle stance by acknowledging the potential that we are able to help people unlock in themselves without placing too much weight on our role in that. In the same breath, we don't want our clients to become attached to us or dependent upon us.

There are so many intricacies that we have to balance in who we are to our clients, that it is vital that we look at ourselves regularly to ensure we haven't got caught in the traps of needing approval or acquiring a heightened sense of grandeur for what we do.

Your Value as a Practitioner

Much of our work together in this book is to help you to recognise the value of you as a practitioner. This also includes the value of you as a teacher, a mentor, somebody people can turn to, and somebody whose services people want. The challenge is that most of us don't see ourselves as an integral part of the choices our clients make. We think they come for our services, but they actually come for us *and* our services. EFT is just a small part of what they come for. Because they also need to be resonating with you in order to invest in you. And you, in turn, need to be resonating with yourself and what you do, because if you don't, you will be giving off the wrong messages. Your potential clients will notice the division in you and they won't buy into working with you.

REFLECTION POINT:

Do you ever see yourself as an integral part of your clients' choices and of life change for them?

Tip: Carry out a swap session with another practitioner. Ask how they benefitted from a session with you. Ask them to be honest. How comfortable were they with you? How safe did they feel to open up? How did they feel you received and worked with their blocks and challenges? Use this as an opportunity to grow as a practitioner, rather than to define your weaknesses. Answer the above questions for them also, and ensure that you give each other feedback on your gifts as well as your growth areas.

On a Level 3 EFT practitioner training, the trainer will often ask a practitioner to demonstrate their skills in front of a group, with the rest of the group giving feedback. The practitioners who are brave enough to receive peer mentoring in this way always grow from the experience. The best thing you can do for your clients is to learn where your weak spots are from your peers, so that you can grow.

IT'S MORE THAN JUST THE OUTCOME

When we carry out an EFT session with someone, the effects are sometimes instantaneous. If someone comes to you with a fear of flying, and by the end of a session or two they can get on an airplane, it is really important for you to recognise how deeply that is going to impact their lives. It isn't just about the plane ride, but what's at the end of the plane ride for them too: being able to travel to business conferences, taking a holiday with their family in an exotic location—these are not trivial things.

Client Experience

A client approached me about her fear of dogs. Her family wanted a puppy. As I took her through the introduction process I conduct with all my clients, I discovered that one of the benefits to her releasing her fear was actually to gain a deeper connection with her son and husband and have more quality time with them, and the puppy was the very thing

> that could help create this. The resolution of the fear was not just to be able to be comfortable around dogs — it was aimed at benefitting the whole family.

We all know the benefits of using these tools and how they impact the lives of others. We've all seen health conditions transformed, phobias disappear, and even conditions such as PTSD and war trauma dramatically impacted. They can cause a certain reverence around EFT which, although rightly due, can make us lose track of our own value and our role in helping others. Again, we don't mean to build it up into something grandiose or make it into an ego-based triumph. But there is still a you in the equation. There is a you who decided to train in these tools, who spent a significant amount of time training in them, practiced them on themselves (and maybe, in the early days, tapped on everything that breathed!).

Of course you don't want to create any heightened sense of grandeur about using the tools. But at the same time, you don't want to be too humble either. Many times I've heard clients thank practitioners and the practitioners reply, "It's not me, it's the tools." However, it is you *and* it is the tools. If you are too humble, you end up missing the chance to fully celebrate what just happened: a powerful combination of EFT, alongside the magic that occurred when you connected with another human being and helped them face their challenges and change them. That is definitely something to be celebrated. If you've been using the response, "It's not me, it's the tools," when your clients thank you, try saying, "You are welcome," or "It's a pleasure," instead, and notice how different the energy is.

Understanding your value is going to help you break your blocks. It's going to help you to design your website, and get your message out to potential clients. When you stand in your own value, your potential clients will find you and know that you are the person they want to be working with, because you, in turn, will know your worth to them.

'Becky'

'Becky', my former fitness instructor, attended a business webinar that I hosted. After the webinar, for feedback, she asked her clients who she was for them. She realised that her marketing wasn't reflecting who she was, and she allowed the question to radically transform how she showed up in business. When I looked at her remodelled website, her adverts in the local newspaper, how she showed up on Facebook and so on, it was apparent that she had truly made use of the answers to this question and then changed the way she showed up. Becky gained a much deeper understanding of what her clients got from her services, and began to understand the true benefits of what she does. Losing weight and getting fit might be the visible results. But the difference that this made to her clients' lives was the real reward. In the introductory calls that she did with clients, her new message became, "I understand you and I understand what you will really gain from this." It is no surprise that when Becky truly began to reflect on what her clients got from her, and to shape her marketing accordingly, her client base increased easily and joyfully.

Summary of Chapter Three

a. **What do you offer your clients?** Ask yourself, "What is it that I actually offer my clients?" Remember, EFT is just part of the equation of what you are offering them. What you are actually offering them is the chance to profoundly change their lives.

b. **When you ask why you are offering these services, the first place you need to look is in you.** What is it that *you* get from using these techniques with others? You need to be able to articulate the value of what you do, so that your clients can connect with that same value.

c. **You need to recognise the value of you as a practitioner, teacher, mentor, somebody people can turn to, and somebody whose services people want.** Most of us don't see ourselves as an integral part of the choices our clients make. We think they come for our services, but they actually come for us *and* our services.

d. **Getting clear on who you are for your clients isn't just for you. It's for them too.** Because if you can confidently know what it is you are deeply offering, then it makes it much easier for your clients to receive it.

e. **As EFT practitioners we offer the opportunity for emotional honesty.** Your clients have to trust you enough in the first place to enable dissolution of the emotional barriers.

f. **As practitioners we have to monitor ourselves when it comes to the amount of emotions we are capable of evoking in people.** We have to ensure that:

    i. We are managing any fears that the session might trigger our own stuff, and our egos as well.

    ii. We have not placed too much weight on our own role in our client's transformation (whilst still valuing what we do).

iii. Our clients don't become attached to us or dependent upon us.

iv. We haven't got caught in the traps of seeking approval or having a heightened sense of grandeur for what we do.

g. **When you look deeper into what your clients are really getting from you, it helps to establish your worth to them and it strengthens the connection between you.** Understanding your value is going to help you break your blocks. It's going to help you to design your website, and get your message out to potential clients.

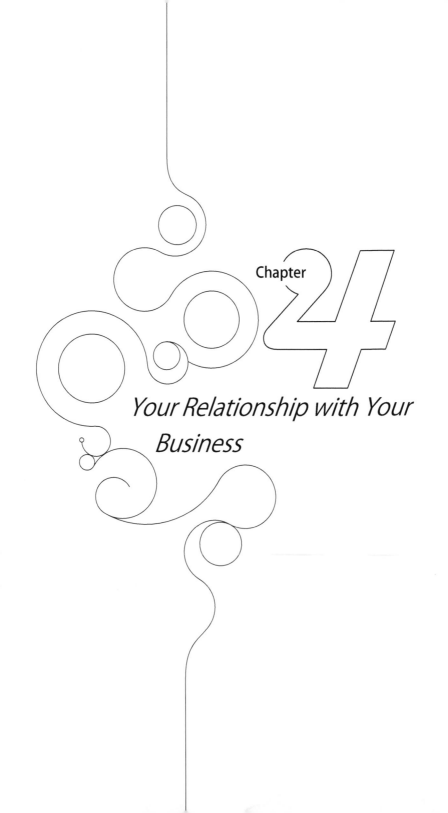

Chapter

4

Your Relationship with Your Business

How you relate to your business today is often highly influenced by what has gone before.

We learn bad habits about how we relate to business from those around us. Maybe your parents or primary caregivers modelled a 'struggling' work ethic, or hated what they did. Perhaps, like most of us, you have taken jobs or set out on career paths that were not suited to you. On some occasions you may have watched the clock and waited for your day to end or for the weekend to come. Without realising it, you may have carried all this into your business through the subconscious, and today you find yourself triggered into old feelings of resentment, even though you love what you do. Then you sit down to do your marketing and you feel like a teenager doing their homework. You struggle against it, and your relationship with your business becomes distant and hostile as a result.

FEELINGS OF INADEQUACY

Any challenges you had previously in life can affect your relationship with your business. Say, for example, you had literacy issues at school or weren't very academic — these issues, and the feelings that accompany them, can be brought forward into your relationship with your business. We're going to cover emotions and beliefs in creating your business in the next chapter, so we won't go into these too deeply right now. But as this is a book for EFT practitioners, it is worth highlighting that any relationship with your business will have an emotional component that will be tinged by your past experiences.

BUSINESS PROGRAMMING

How did your parents and primary caregivers respond to their work or business? We learn how to respond and relate to work and business from those around us. If your caregivers thrived and had a healthy relationship with work and money, it is likely you will bring this forward. If the opposite was true, it is likely that you will have some tapping to do (and again, we will look at this in more depth in the next chapter).

A friend of mine, 'Tara', who has had a successful business for over a decade, shared with me how different her perception filters are around business and finance to those of her partner. Her partner, 'Saman', grew up in post-war Iran. There was a lot of poverty in the country at the time and the children had next to nothing. On a really good day they might get a football to kick about between them. They got one new outfit a year, and on the dinner table there were often only two small cubes of meat on each plate.

Tara grew up in the North of England and also had a lot of financial challenges. Although her father was well paid, he had numerous accidents throughout his life, which meant there was also a scarcity of food at times (but definitely not as significant as in post-war Iran).

So, which one of them ended up with the biggest challenges around money and finance to clear? You may be surprised to hear that it was Tara, and not Saman. The difference was their fathers' relationship to work and money. Saman's father taught his children that money problems were the best kind of problems to have, because they were solvable. Even though there was not much to go around, he had a knack of being very creative with their resources and he did not model fear about money and finances to his children. As an adult, Saman took on the same traits. He became a highly successful businessman and entrepreneur because he always had a creative relationship with money and finance.

Tara was also highly successful. However, she had a lot of work to do to overcome her pattern of getting triggered when business was on a downturn. She would easily get triggered into scarcity, just as her father did at these times and the consequence was that her creativity plunged to a very low level because she was swept into survival mode (something we shall also explore in the chapter on money). She had to reprogramme her response from, "Money problems are the worst kind of problems you can have," to a mindset that was more in line with her partner's. Fortunately with tools such as EFT (and also using the advanced EFT tool Matrix Reimprinting), she was able to rewrite her old programmes and get creative, instead of going into a freeze response when there were financial hurdles to overcome.

EXERCISE: YOUR BUSINESS PROGRAMMING

What have you learnt about work, money and business from the people around you? How are those patterns affecting how you relate to your business today?

Tune in to the feeling or the belief statement that is associated with those patterns and start slowly tapping. Close your eyes and allow your mind to bring to your awareness memories related to this issue and identify the earliest.

Check in to see if you took on a belief that was not your own (which is usually the case). You can simply ask where the energy came from and then return it with love, consciousness and awareness attached. Alternatively, you can use your preferred method of rewriting a memory or taking the charge out of it.

You can also visualise yourself in a comfortable and light place, and bring in front of you, one at a time, each person that has had a negative impact on the way you relate to work or business.

Notice how you feel about them. If you feel uncomfortable at any point, stop and tap to clear the accompanying issues.

Discuss with each person where the belief came from and where they are still holding the emotion of the energy of the belief. With their permission, tap on them (or bring someone in to tap on them) to release any negative emotion attached to their belief.

As the energy transforms, check in with how you are both feeling. If the belief or learning is generational, send this new positive energy up and down the generational timeline for both of you.

Also, start to send this energy to the area that is connected to your work, money and business. For example, allow the positive energy to flow through you, your computer, your desk, your chairs, your business cards, your website, and so on.

Now visualise yourself in the future. With this new energy and new feeling, what would you be doing? How would you be feeling? Visualise a picture any time in the near or distant future. Tune into the positive feelings of your future self.

Send the new picture through the top of your head, around your body and out through your heart.

Repeat this process for every person you had a learning from around money, business or finance.

'Ellen'

'Ellen' has a successful international business. She also places her spirituality as being high on her agenda for life. A meditator and practitioner of yoga, she describes herself as having been on some kind of spiritual path for the last twenty years.

She came to me because she perceived her business to be something separate from her spirituality. She identified business as being on her right side and spirituality as being on her left side. When she stood to the left of herself, she described her spiritual experience as being light, free, expansive, open, and so on. When she stood to the right of herself, she described the energy of her business to be duty-bound, heavy, restricting, and so on. Even though she had had a successful business for years, energetically, her perception of it was weighing her down. Only by bringing these two energies together was she able to bring her spiritual experience into her business realm, and the result was more enthusiasm for her work and more presence when she was working.

YOUR BUSINESS IDENTITY

If your business had an identity, what would it be? It could be a person, an object, an animal, etc.

When we place identities on to, say money or business or objects in our life, we can work in a much more creative and dynamic way with them.

I developed this exercise as part of the *Realise Your Dreams* programme and it was subsequently featured in *Transform your Beliefs, Transform Your Life* (the new Matrix Reimprinting book by Karl Dawson and Kate Marillat).

Picturing your business in this way is a great way of working with your subconscious. The subconscious thinks in pictures and these pictures enable you to converse with your business, gauge your own feelings towards it, and also know how it is feeling towards you! You can also keep checking in and identifying growth, challenges and changes.

When I picture my business, it is a globe with arms and legs. Some of the examples given by clients and course participants include a puppy, a clown, a lion, a red hat with opening arms, a goddess, a plant and a tree.

EXERCISE: YOUR BUSINESS AS AN OBJECT

This is a great 'check in' exercise and relationship builder between you and your business. It is designed to help you tune in to your subconscious thoughts about your business and connect with your business self at a deeper level.

Close your eyes and picture your business as an object, animal or person.

Step into the picture with your business. This works best if you are associated (fully in your body rather than looking at the picture from the outside).

Introduce yourself to your business.
How do you feel being in the presence of your business? What emotions is it bringing up for you? Tap through any negative emotions that are coming up for you.

Once you have reduced the emotions, ask your business identity, "How are you feeling towards me?" See what emotions come up.

Does your business need tapping? If so, you can do this yourself on your business or have another imaginary figure (such as a spiritual figure, someone who is already successful in business, etc.) come in to the picture and tap on your business for you.

Also remember to tap on yourself if this brings up negative emotions for you.

Take time to connect with your business. Say what you need to say and listen to what your business says.

Ask your business what it needs of you. Ask yourself what you need from your business.

How can you support each other? How can you two build a better relationship together? How can you move forward as a team?

Agree on an action step to grow your relationship. This may be a physical action or an energetic clearing. Thank your business for showing up in this way and arrange a time to meet to talk together again.

Step out of the picture and look at it from the outside. Borrowing a process from the advanced EFT tapping tool Matrix Reimprinting, the next step is to reimprint the picture. To do this, tap as you send the picture through the top of your head, allowing all the neurons in your brain to reconnect with the information about your new relationship with your business. Next send it around your cells and into your heart. Use your heart to send it out into the universe in every direction, rewriting everything that you previously knew (consciously or otherwise) about your business.

Now look at your relationship with your business again and note what has changed on an energetic level.

Ensure you carry out the action step you agreed on and make a regular point to connect with your business in this way. It is useful to make a weekly appointment in your diary to connect with your business identity. This will enable growth and development as a relationship and highlight any limitations and growth opportunities.

The following statements are initial feedback from my clients about this exercise:
"I can't rely on my business, I don't have enough

time with you, I feel amazing when we work together, but empty and abandoned when it doesn't work out. My happiness depends on you and I am giving away my power to you."

"Meeting my business, I just heard, 'More, more, more. Release us from our chains.' And I'm thinking the chains are the blocks and limiting beliefs."

"My business was feeling neglected. It wants me to work with a colleague and make a vision board and get to know it better through a right-brain activity."

"My business was a lion. It was tied up and felt pitiful. Angels came to support it and it wanted me to walk my talk."

"My business is a goddess and we are now standing side by side with my arm around her. We may need an admin assistant so we can expand."

"My business told me it needs feeding and to stop hiding it out in the woods. It likes it there. It's calm and peaceful, but it's time to be seen. We need to get to know each other."

"My business was a clown and it was amazing. It could juggle a lot of balls, carry out numerous tricks and zoom about all over the place. It told me that it had so much more potential than what I was currently creating and there was lots of fast-paced and exciting action to be had if I would just allow it. This exercise helped me get really clear and unapologetic about getting my message out there."

Recognising the importance of creating a relationship with your business, overcoming past programming about working relationships and checking in and communicating with your business regularly will enable it to flourish and grow more readily.

Summary of Chapter Four

a. **We learn bad habits about how we relate to business from those around us.** We also take old incidents of struggle that we learnt previously into our current business relationship.

b. **Any challenges you had previously in life, such as literacy issues, can affect your relationship with your business.** Addressing these will vastly affect the way you show up in business.

c. **If your business had an identity, what would it be?** It could be a person, an object, an animal, and so on. When we place identities on money or business or objects in our life, it enables us to work in a much more creative and dynamic way with them.

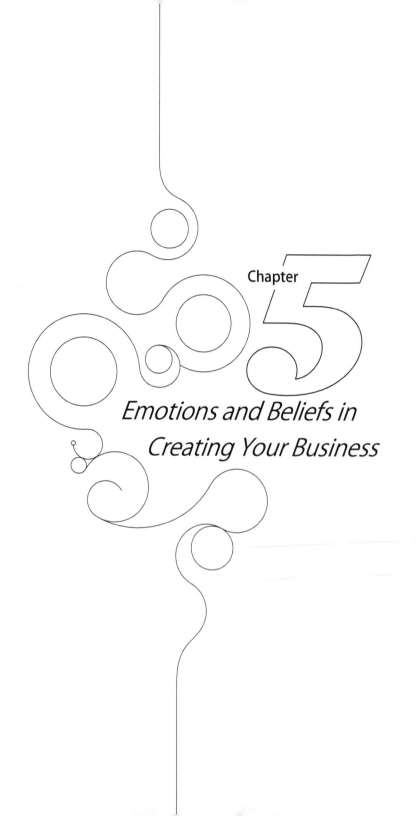

Chapter

5

Emotions and Beliefs in
Creating Your Business

The only thing standing in the way of how great your business can be is <u>you</u>.

This can be really tough to swallow, but it is meant as a call to action rather than something to trigger you into thoughts of failure.

The truth is, your business is going to be as great as you perceive it is going to be. And the more your limited perception gets in the way of your greatness, the more challenges you are going to have to overcome to line yourself up emotionally with that which you are creating.

As we highlighted in Chapter 1, the best way to create a fulfilling and rewarding business is to create it in the context of the life that you love.

You are building your business in the context of family relationships, old friendships, new connections, and holidays you want to take. You have a life and you also have a business, but there's a key point in this which is you. All the above elements are part of you, extensions of you, and your business is an extension too. Therefore, when you are putting energy into new ventures for your business, these new ventures are also extensions of who you are. And precisely because all these extensions are interconnected, and an integral part of you, as you go about your business activities, your unresolved issues can be triggered and you can get blocked.

Many people I coach find that they didn't have the same kind of emotions coming up when they were working for someone else. Perhaps you have been in a situation where you turned up, did your job, and were not emotionally tied to being there. Whereas when you have your own business, you're putting you out in the world. You wouldn't choose to start a business if you weren't passionate about what you were doing. You wouldn't be reading this book if you weren't passionate about the services that you want to bring to the world. And all this passion gets tied up emotionally with the entity known as your business, along with your fears, hopes and dreams. There is no wonder that it seems overwhelming at times.

EMOTIONAL OVERWHELM AND FEAR ABOUT STARTING

Emotional overwhelm is actually one of the most common patterns that gets triggered at this time. Sometimes fear, frustration, anxiety and anger are thrown into the mix. You have so many roles to juggle and a number of new skills to learn. You have to do your own public relations, market your business, do your accounts, carry out your admin, and so on. In addition, you may have to learn new tech skills and build a website. Even something as seemingly trivial as putting a PayPal button on your website can take hours to learn.

When all that is underway, you might actually get to do the bit that you really love and spur people on to transform their lives! But if you get frustrated and are held back by all the new skills you need to learn and apply, you can end up procrastinating about work and putting everything off for another day.

Procrastination

Often in business we can procrastinate without realising why we are doing so. As a result, procrastination can become a measure by which we judge ourselves. "I've dreamed of setting up my own business my whole life and now I have found what I love, I am procrastinating." However, procrastination isn't something to shame yourself with. Instead, it is usually a product of overwhelm.

It's easy for us to feel that because we have the tools of EFT, we should be able to tap ourselves out of procrastination. I've found that it isn't that simple for a lot of my clients. I've heard them say, "I've got the best tools in the world at my disposal but I can't tap my way out of procrastination. How can I inspire clients if I can't inspire myself?" If this has been your story, you are not alone. Undoubtedly you have tried "Even though I am procrastinating, I deeply love and accept myself." But without answering the deeper why of your procrastination, you aren't able to identify the root cause so you can tap on it and transform it.

This kind of procrastination often leads us to shut down or become defensive. Instead of rising to the challenge, many of us say, "You know, that's not my skill," or "That's not what I'm about; I'm not going to do it." We dig our heels in and, without the financial backing to hire someone to do these things for us, we reach a stalemate. I've been there myself, and it is very frustrating.

Yet there are so many opportunities that are missed when we are in overwhelm. In this phase I have often heard clients saying, "That's it! I'm getting a job at the supermarket." This is a common stock response to having to deal with these challenges. I've even said it myself a couple of times, when the website I've been building is malfunctioning or something technological is not working. I am all too familiar with that feeling of being pushed over the edge and crying out like this.

REFLECTION POINT:

Have you ever felt overwhelmed by your business? Have you felt fear and anxiety? Have you, like me, felt anger rising within you when you try to do the tasks that you don't have the skill set (and sometimes the passion) for?

EXERCISE: Sit quietly and identify the emotions coming up.
Rate the intensity on a scale of 1-10 and start tapping. Where do these emotions lead you? Where is the fear based? What are the memories or mind chatter coming through?

> Use the Movie Technique or Matrix Reimprinting with memories that come up. Then re-evaluate the intensity from 1-10. Keep working through them one by one.

HOW EMOTIONS AFFECT CLIENT ATTRACTION

When you feel overwhelmed and frustrated, it's not really the kind of place from which you feel inspired to go and find new clients to work with. In these moments, your business is in a place of contraction rather than expansion. As soon as you hit the question of "Where do I start and what do I do?", if you don't have a creative answer or aren't able to break it down into manageable pieces, it can be easier to just walk away and say, "I'm just not doing it today." If that's the energy you are generating behind your business, then even if you do get inquiries from prospective clients, they may pick up on your underlying emotions, subconsciously or otherwise, and decide not to work with you.

In contrast, when you are able to move beyond some of those frustrating emotions that are keeping you locked in a holding pattern of not doing anything, your whole energy around your business will change. Often it is just a matter of getting clearer about what you are offering. I've lost count of the number of times a client has told me that they are frustrated because they can't do their website. After I ask them a series of questions, what they discover is that it's not about writing copy for their website: it's that they aren't clear enough on what they are offering.

Some of my questions are:
• "What kind of clients do you want to work with?"

- "Why would they be coming to you?"
- "What are you offering them?"
- "Do you have enough knowledge about what you are doing?"
- "Have you practiced enough to feel competent?"

If you don't know what your message is (something we will explore in Chapter 6), then how can you communicate it succinctly to your clients?

Many times we can't answer these questions right away. We might have a vague idea of whom we want to work with but we need to do a few sessions with people in order to get really clear. We think we want to work with big-T trauma, but after working with some really challenging cases we realise that doing that might be too intense for us on a day-to-day basis. Alternatively, we find that we have an unexpected skill set working with another issue, such as phobias. I've worked with practitioners who really love the gritty issues such as trauma, and others that are more suited to working with confidence, beliefs or weight loss issues. If you have not really thought about whom you are serving and what their specific needs are, when you sit down to write your marketing copy, it is likely that your message will be fragmented and unclear.

Fear

Of course, frustration isn't the only emotional state you are likely to encounter as you are setting out. You may also experience fear. This can include fear about whether you will actually get any clients or not, or fear that you don't actually know where you are going to find them (which can leave you feeling like you have to pull the rabbit out of the hat). Then there is also the fear of what will happen if you don't get them; this can include how you are going to pay the rent, bills, mortgage, etc. A further fear can arise which is: "If I do get clients, will I actually know what to do with them?"

All these fears can snowball, and then you find yourself sitting at your desk thinking, "I don't want to do my website," and so on. But it's not really about the website, but a deeper emotional feeling — something we are all too familiar with in our work with EFT!

EXERCISE: OVERCOMING FEARS AND FRUSTRATIONS

Make an inventory of all the fears and frustrations you have experienced so far in your business. Many of them won't be conscious, so use the above examples to check in with yourself and see where these emotions are strongest for you.

Take a twofold approach to addressing your fears and frustrations by dealing with them on both an energetic and a practical level.

Energetic Level: These are based on your perceptions or life experiences. They are your tappable issues. Work through them by yourself or with a swap partner.

Your Offering: What are you offering and who are you serving? For example, you may find yourself saying, "I'm still not sure what kind of clients I would like to work with or what my specialism is," or "I don't know what my core message is for my clients," etc. This book is going to help you get really clear on these kinds of questions, but it helps if you become aware if you are not clear at this point. Remember to tap on any emotion that comes up when you are thinking about your offering.

Knowledge and Experience: Identify any knowledge or experience that you need to gain. For example, do you need to do some more swap sessions in order to build up your skill set? Do you need to do some more study so that you can articulate what you do more effectively? (Also note that many of the clients I work with run the belief, "I don't know enough," or "I am not skilled enough." It fuels the course junkie in us. Check in with yourself if it's really true that you need to know more, or if you are hiding behind this belief so you can resist putting yourself out there.)

Practical Level: Do you need to create your own website, learn how to put a PayPal button on your site, learn how to create an email list, master Facebook, etc.? Perhaps you are further along your journey and ready to host webinars and online training programmes. Unless you have the luxury of hiring someone to do these things, make a list of them in order of importance. Don't try to do them all at once! Instead, take them one at a time, in order of priority. Remember, there are demonstrations on YouTube for practically every single thing you need to learn online, so tackle them one at a time, and as soon as you feel any frustration, stop and tap.

Now that you have a practical plan for moving through some of the frustrations you have been facing, hopefully it feels more manageable. We will build on this plan as the book progresses.

Also, the very act of sitting down, focusing and

> writing down the above enables you to look for the underlying beliefs and emotions such as "I am out of my depth," "Who do I think I am by trying to do this?", "Why would anyone come to me?" and so on.

How Beliefs Affect Client Attraction

It isn't only our day-to-day frustrations around clarity, knowledge and technological skills that can affect how we show up for clients. It's our beliefs too. If you are running beliefs such as "I am invisible," for example, your clients aren't going to be able to see or hear you. In addition, you probably don't want to be seen in the world either, so it becomes a catch-22. There is a huge longing to take your work out into the world, but the belief is often stronger, so you find yourself living divided and a battle ensues between your heart's desire and your core belief. In such cases, we often find ourselves projecting onto our prospective clients and asking, "Why is nobody seeing me?"

EXERCISE:

Tune into your body and see if any of the following beliefs about business are currently true for you. Rate each one from 0-10, with 0 being 'No truth in that at all,' and 10 being 'That is totally true for me.'
» It's hard work.
» I can't do it.
» I'm not good enough.
» I don't know what to do.
» I'm just not capable.
» Clients don't just turn up.
» I'm insignificant.
» I'm invisible.
» I'm not a good practitioner.

» I have to get it right.
» Something bad is going to happen if I get it wrong.
» The clients will only come if .... (For example: 'I'm perfect.')
» People would take advantage of me.
» I don't have any boundaries.
» I'm not recognised.

Now, take one belief at a time starting with the most significant one and note:

- Where you feel it resonating
- How you would describe the feeling
- What colour, shape or object you would associate it with
- What the emotion is that is connected to the feeling. These are all tappable issues. You may choose to work through them on your own, or alternatively with a swap partner or another practitioner.

If you are tapping on yourself, start with the belief, notice where you feel it in your body, and with your eyes closed, begin tapping. You may find an original memory or series of memories linked to this belief that you can use the Movie Technique to resolve.

Personally, I've seen people have great results with the advanced EFT tool Matrix Reimprinting, because it helps you to go back to where the beliefs were formed and rewrite them (rather than just taking the negative charge out of them as with conventional EFT). (See *Resources* for where to learn more about Matrix Reimprinting.)

The following comments are from participants of the *Realise Your Magical Business* programme, which was hosted by myself and Sharon King:

'Matthew' found himself resonating with, "It's hard work," and he felt annoyed with himself for feeling that way.

'Amy' went with "I'm not good enough" and she felt it in her stomach at a seven.

'Alisa' said people will take advantage of her and it was a level nine.

'Jane' had a nine or a ten on being insignificant.

'Janice' said that "I can't do it," "I'm not good enough," and "I have to get it right," all resonated with her. In her stomach she felt "control" and it was jammed up like cement.

'Barry' said, "I'm not recognised," which was a level six in his chest.

'Paula' was afraid to be seen, at a level eight.

I share these with you as they are practitioners, just like you, and hopefully seeing other people's responses will do two things. Firstly, reassure you that you are not alone and secondly, empower you to get to the root of your beliefs and change them using EFT.

So, with these belief systems going on within you, it's going to be hard for clients to say: "Yes, you are the person I want to work with," when your energy is saying "Oh no, I'm not good enough," "It's hard work," or "Clients won't come if I haven't done this or that!" It's not exactly a warm or inviting energy for clients to cosy up to!

Working through the Issues that Arise

One important note before we close this chapter. It would be easy for you to go into overwhelm when you start reading this book, especially if you realise there is a lot of tapping to be done. The idea isn't to get yourself to a place of perfection and then start your business. The idea is to start your business with the understanding of the work you have to do and allow yourself to develop on the journey.

Most of the successful practitioners that I know, myself included, started when there were still some challenges to overcome. When I started my practice, I was still recovering from chronic fatigue syndrome, deep in debt and a smoker with an eating disorder. I know practitioners who started their practice while they were still recovering from depression; one practitioner with MS was working with people from her wheelchair, and other practitioners were trying to lose weight, quit smoking, and had a whole variety of other hang-ups.

So the point is, don't wait until you are a perfect version of yourself to start, because if you are hiding behind an ideal of where you think a practitioner should be before they start, you will miss the opportunity to help people. But at the same time, see yourself as a work in progress as you go along, defining and transforming your underlying issues so you can show up as present as possible for your clients, without letting your past weigh you down to the point where you don't get your business started. Your clients will trigger your unresolved issues, but you will grow faster if you have your sleeves up and are ready to face your issues in the process.

Summary of Chapter Five

a. **The only thing standing in the way of how great your business can be is <u>you</u>.** Your business is going to be as great as you perceive it is going to be.

b. **Emotional overwhelm is actually one of the most common patterns that gets triggered in new business owners.** It can lead to procrastination. It is vital that you don't shame yourself with procrastination.

c. **When you feel overwhelmed and frustrated, it can negatively affect client attraction.** In contrast, when you are able to move beyond some of those frustrating emotions that are keeping you locked in a holding pattern of not doing anything, your whole energy around your business will change.

d. **You may also experience fear when you first set out.** This can prevent you from taking practical action.

e. **Your limiting beliefs about yourself and the world also affect client attraction.** Transforming any limiting beliefs will enable you to feel better about being in business and will also mean you attract more clients.

Chapter 6

Creating Your Unique
Message

Your message is the heartbeat of your business.

A well-defined message speaks to your customers in a way that ignites their confidence in what you do. It tells them that you know who you are and what you stand for. Yet for many of my clients, when I ask them what their message is, they draw a blank. Others give me a textbook answer (often one that focuses solely on the benefits of EFT). Such an answer is often void of the passion that they have for the work that they do.

The main point to understand is that your unique selling point (USP) is *you*. As we highlighted previously in Chapter 2, you are the unique element of your business that exists outside of the tools. The tools themselves are nothing without the person that uses them. The way you show up in the world, your passion and your enthusiasm for what you do, how you relate what you do to what your clients need — that is your USP.

However, the challenge is that many of us don't think about shaping our unique message to what our audience actually wants. The single biggest mistake I see practitioners make is that they shape their message around the techniques that they practice. Your prospective clients are less interested in the techniques you are practicing and more interested in the results they are going to get from working with you specifically. Your clients are seeking you out because they want results, and your unique message needs to be a reflection of this.

If you have been focusing on the tools you use over what your clients are going to gain from working with you, then you're definitely not alone. You can search through a number of EFT websites on the market to see what I mean. Quite often you will land on the homepage and see a history of EFT, a picture of the tapping points, and so on. In contrast, some marketing experts say that you shouldn't even mention the tools you use on your site. They say you should make your site specifically about your audience's needs and how you are going to meet them. We'll discuss whether or not it is relevant to include a description of EFT on your own site later in this chapter, but for now, our focus is defining a message that connects with your audience rather than one that describes what you do.

THE FOUNDATION QUESTIONS

In Chapter 3 we began to explore who you are to your clients. The following exercise will enable you to define how you shape who you are to your clients into a message that will help them to understand what you are offering them.

> **EXERCISE:**
>
> 1. Write down five reasons why your clients will be looking for your services.
> 2. What are five reasons why your clients may choose the tools and techniques that you use?
> 3. Write down five benefits your clients will receive from your sessions.
> 4. How will you benefit your clients? Write down five benefits your clients will receive from specifically working with you.
> 5. What is it you love about the services you offer? Not specifically what you love about EFT, but more what you love about the results you get.

The more information you can generate about what you're doing and why you're doing it, the better. Your answers along with your purpose statement are going to sit at the heart of your marketing and client generation. This exercise will not only help you to build your website—it will also enable you to tune into your passion.

When you have this information, it will enable you to more effectively communicate through the spoken and written word. Whether you are writing emails, blogs or copy for your website, speaking about your services at networking meetings, or recording video or audio, you are going to be connecting more with what you do. It will also enable you to introduce yourself very simply and authentically to people in a very short space of time. For example, one of my friends highlighted how she made an instant decision to hire a marketing advisor right at the start of her practitioner career. She met her at a networking event and the marketing advisor simply stated, "Hi, I'm Lisa, and I enable and facilitate practitioners to get more clients that they are passionate about working with." She knew how to speak to what my friend was looking for, or in other words, her needs.

NICHING

One of the most frequent questions I get asked by my clients is whether they should be a specialist or a generalist. Niching can push all kinds of buttons in people. Although we are often generally advised to niche, and told that it is better to be a specialist than a generalist, I offer an alternative view about niching to my clients.

The challenge is, sometimes the very idea of niching stunts the growth of the business. What I've seen time and time again is practitioners hearing that they have to niche and then deciding not to market themselves until they have.

To get stuck on niching is a form of procrastination. Because if you aren't out there in the world doing the work you love, how do you work out what your niche is? Your niche grows with you, rather than being something you come up with in your head.

So if you already have a niche that feels aligned to you, feel free to stay with it. But if you don't, work through the questions on your purpose and others you've seen in this book so far, so you get your key words for what you are offering to clients. When you define what you are offering, it enables you to 'niche' while still remaining a generalist. Instead of working with a specific group on a fixed issue, you make the uniqueness of what you are offering into your niche.

This is how I developed my own area, Realise Your Dreams. It isn't a niche like weight loss or working with athletes. However, I had much more success putting myself out like that than I did working with health clients. When I first marketed myself as someone who helped others realise their dreams, I began earning £5,000 per month through clients alone. This is much more than I was earning as a "Health Specialist", even though I was somewhat of an expert in working with health conditions. (And of course, I had moved into doing the work I truly loved, rather than the work I felt obliged to do.)

If you think about it, because you know how to work with emotions, you are already a specialist! So the journey with niching is twofold. Firstly, get beyond any fear you have about niching and secondly, create a message that reflects your own, unique offering. This includes your core values, purpose statements and so on. The words that resonate with you become the ones that come through in your message. *That* becomes your niche.

Do You Have Enough Knowledge for Your Chosen Field?

If you are niching in a particular area, one consideration is that you have enough knowledge and experience in your field to specialise. If you have had a similar transformation yourself in the field that you are choosing to specialise in, it is often more preferable to clients than having learnt your subject from a book or training course. Your own transformation can be pivotal to your specialism, and we will discuss this later in this chapter when we examine the story behind your brand.

If You Are Still Considering Niching

If you are considering niching, either you have a niche at this point or you are open to discovering what it might be. If it is the latter, one of two things is going to happen. You are going to find your niche or your niche is going to find you. Often, after doing a series of sessions with clients, you will find yourself gravitating towards the ones that you are most resonant to working with. Alternatively, numerous people will start asking you to help them with a specific issue, and you will realise it is your specialism.

One important note though. You might still decide that you don't want to have a niche and choose to remain a general practitioner. In this case, I want to reiterate that it is vital that you have really defined and owned the uniqueness of what you do. If you are a generalist, you have to ensure that you have defined your unique qualities and are standing by them. Otherwise you will definitely get lost in the sea of others who are doing something similar. Especially if you have decided to generalise, you have to have defined your USP as you. One of the ways you can do this is sharing the story behind what you do.

THE STORY BEHIND YOUR BRAND

Why did you get into EFT in the first place? Perhaps, like me, you were one of EFT's miracles, turning yourself around from a debilitating health condition or serious disease. Maybe you lost a ton of weight or overcame a lifelong fear or phobia. You might have gathered newfound confidence or transformed social anxiety or a general feeling of not belonging in the world. Alternatively, perhaps you experienced a big-T trauma, and were able to get back out in the world without the stress symptoms you used to exhibit frequently.

On the other hand, your journey with EFT might have been more subtle. Maybe you started out as one of EFT's doubters or sceptics, but found yourself won over when you saw the effects of the results on yourself and others. Perhaps your transformation was slower and more incremental, as you saw small shifts and changes in the way you related to yourself and others.

Whatever your story with EFT, it is valuable to your potential clients because it connects them to you. It helps them to meet the human behind the tools. And let's face it, if you are asking them to feel comfortable about opening up to you emotionally, then you want to ensure that you are someone who is approachable. You would be amazed at how many clients I have had over the years who said something along the lines of: "As soon as I read your story I knew I needed to connect with you." The following will enable you to share your story skilfully.

Sharing the Story Behind Your Brand

- Have a separate page on your website called 'About (your name)'. Remember, fundamentally you want your site to be about them and not about you, so don't mix your story up with your offering.
- Ensure you show some form of vulnerability. Refer to different emotional states that you overcame, particularly how you felt before your transformation and afterwards. Emotion connects you to your potential client.

- Make sure you don't spill out emotionally. Although this might appear to contradict what I have just said, there is a difference between you sharing how you felt in the past and you joining your client in the pain of where they are now. It is helpful if you can share a (mostly) healed story with them. If you are right in the middle of transforming the issue they are coming to you with, it might not be as strong a message as if you were writing from a healed place.

> **EXERCISE:**
>
> Write your 'Story Behind My Brand' using the above guidelines. It will probably require several edits before you get it right. Make sure you lead in with an impactful opening line to draw the readers in. (See my story on page xx.) Ask someone you trust (who also knows your field well) to give you feedback on it. Also, ask someone who fits the description of your ideal client for feedback. Did it connect with them emotionally? Did they feel they could trust you after reading it? Did they feel that you have an understanding of their journey?

Fears About Sharing Your Story

Many of my clients freeze when I encourage them to write the story behind their brand. It is actually an incredibly vulnerable thing that I am asking you to do by putting your own personal story out there. In conventional therapy, it would be considered unprofessional to share an aspect of our life story with our clients. Yet in EFT, the rules change because you are down on the ground with your clients, often tapping on yourself and them simultaneously. It is much more personal, in many ways, than some of the more conventional forms of therapy.

During much of your professional life you have probably been taught to wear a mask and hide your feelings. Yet in EFT, you learn the opposite. It can take a shift in perception to learn to be skilfully emotionally available for your clients. It's not one that is learnt overnight.

However, if the mere thought of sharing your story triggers you, then there is still work to do. Refer back to Chapter 5 on emotions and beliefs in creating your business. Any underlying fears about being seen or exposed that haven't been dealt with yet will definitely trigger when you start to write the story behind your brand.

Your story is part of your connection and demonstrates to clients:
a.   That you understand where they currently are
b.   That you overcame stuff too
c.   The benefits that you experienced
d.   The benefits others have received
e.   Your purpose and reason for working with them.

Summary of Chapter Six

a.   **A well-defined message speaks to your customers in a way that ignites their confidence in what you do.** It lets them see that you know who you are and what you stand for.
b.   **Your unique selling point is *you*.** You are the unique element of your business, and that exists outside of the tools.
c.   **Many of us don't think about shaping our unique message to what our audience actually wants.** The single biggest mistake I see practitioners make is that

they shape their message around the techniques that they practice. Your clients are seeking you out because they want results, and your unique message needs to be a reflection of this.

d.   **The more information you can generate about what you're doing and why you're doing it, the better.** Ensure that you know what your clients get from working with you.

e.   **You might decide that you don't want to have a niche, and choose to remain a general practitioner.** In this case, it is vital that you have really defined and owned the uniqueness of what you do.

f.   **Your own story with EFT is valuable to your potential clients because it connects them to you.** It helps them to meet the human behind the tools. Ensure you tap on any fears you have to sharing the story behind your brand.

Chapter

7

Developing Your Presence

When we first hear that we have to develop 'presence' in our business, it can sound like something mystical. However, developing presence is far more practical than it might seem. Presence is simply letting people know that your business exists. When you develop your presence, your prospective clients are able to learn how your services and skill set could be of benefit to them. Your presence is the way that you show people that you can help them (or help others that they know).

BUILDING PRESENCE

Just as with all your aspects of business building, presence can be built skilfully or unskilfully. To build your presence skilfully means to create regular communication with your potential or existing clients. You build trust and understanding by showing that you are available and by allowing them to see that communicating with you is joyful and easy.

Your presence needs to invite your potential clients to have a dialogue with you. This is a skill in itself and something that is often learnt through trial and error. The challenge is that if you don't make yourself available for dialogue, your clients are less likely to purchase from you. On the other hand, if you open yourself wide to a dialogue that involves countless communications back and forth between your clients before they invest in you, you leave yourself wide open to boundary issues with your clients at a later date. It may mean that that same "it's free for all" presence which you showed up with at the start of your connection is carried into the working relationship. In such a case you may find yourself dealing with a never-ending stream of communication from your client when you start working together. This is where presence without boundaries can become problematic.

The other side to this is that we can end up closing ourselves off because we are afraid that our clients will want too much from us. In such cases, our presence can seem more like a monologue. We are out there sharing our message, but there is no invitation for our clients to engage in the conversation with us before they invest in us. In such cases they are less likely to invest. It is said that people are most likely to do business with those they know, like and trust. Your presence can go a long way towards your potential clients knowing you and liking you. However, in order to trust you there often needs to be a more personal interaction. This is something that reassures them that engaging with you is going to feel comfortable. This is why practitioners often offer a free, 20-minute, no obligation consultation before clients commit to them.

So connection with clients is about communication and understanding. In the old paradigm of business, presence used to be about "Here I am and this is what I do!" The new paradigm is more akin to "Here we both are, this is what I do, and how can it be of service to you and your challenges?"

In the old paradigm, you could put an advert out and customers would roll in. But priorities have changed, especially with the advent of social media. Have you ever stopped to ask yourself this very basic question: "Why is Facebook so popular?" For most of us it became so entrenched in our lives that we didn't even consider the question. And the answer, although it seems obvious, is at the heart of what forms the new paradigm in business. People use Facebook because they like to connect. Many people aren't receiving the same sense of community in their personal environments as the generations before them did, so they look to social media to fill that gap. In the same way, when they consider investing in you, they look for where and how to connect. And if they don't feel met by your business presence, it is unlikely they will reach out to purchase your services.

WHO DO YOU THINK YOU NEED TO BE?

Another aspect that has changed significantly, particularly in the personal development industry, is showing your audience your human side. In the old paradigm of business, a leader in the self-help industry needed to have the presence of a warrior. There was a trend for leaders in the field to put on a front to their audience, only revealing what they had transformed in their lives and keeping under wraps the issues that they were still working with. Often there was a pedestal-based relationship, which caused more damage than good. It made their audience feel like there was somewhere to get to and they hadn't arrived yet. Thankfully, this kind of ego-based leadership has dwindled and it has become more fashionable to show your human side. Again, this is a skill. Spill your emotions out everywhere and your clients will not feel safe to go to you. Keep too guarded and your clients will not build the trust component or relate to you on a human level.

Maintaining regular, authentic contact with your potential clients boosts their confidence in you. It reinforces your name and services in their awareness and even if they don't require your services at this time, they will be able to recall your name or service to their friends because of the trust they have built in you.

WAYS TO CREATE PRESENCE

There are numerous ways to create presence. I would suggest that you choose more than one, but don't try to do them all at once (a mistake that many new business owners make, leaving that familiar feeling of overwhelm).

They include:

- Websites
- Blogs
- Newsletters
- Teleclasses / webinars
- Flyers
- Interviews
- Press releases
- Magazine articles
- Presentations / talks
- Podcasts
- Social Media profiles

YOUR WEBSITE

Your website is a great way of letting your clients know who you are and what you do. It's an online presence that anybody can find at any time, so it works to develop your presence 24/7.

If you are looking at enabling your clients to find you over the Internet, a website is crucial. It also gives you tools and functions that can support your business. Most practitioners who are setting up understand the importance of building a website. Remember how we highlighted earlier that people are likely to purchase from those they know, like and trust? A website is crucial for people to see you as someone who is committed to their business.

Yet many new practitioners panic when they hear the word 'website'. Perhaps you've experienced something similar. If you've already built your website, that panic probably feels like a distant memory. But if you are just starting out, that panic can feel very real.

The good news is that nowadays, websites are affordable to set up, and it is much easier to build one than it was when I first went into business.

Purpose of Your Website

Your first step (this is useful to do even if you currently have a website) is to identify the purpose of your website. Before you start putting things online or trying to build something, ask yourself what you actually want the site to do for you. In the same vein as when we asked you what your purpose is in business, you need to know what your website is going to do for your business.

Is it to have people contact you directly about your services? Are you looking for people to pick up the phone or write you an email to be able to talk to you about your services? Would you like to create a community? Perhaps you'd like to use your website to share knowledge.

One warning here though. If you share too much knowledge upfront on your website, any call to action you want your clients to take in order to reach out to you might get lost in the sea of information. It's important to distinguish between websites that share lots of information and those that inform about services. You can do both, but it needs to be skilfully done so your services don't get lost in the process.

Whatever type of website you have, it is vital that it have the facility to build a list of interested people who may become your clients in the future.

> **Ask yourself:** What do I want my website to do for me in the next 12-24 months? How can it best serve me and my clients?

Your website is important because it is sometimes the first and only opportunity for you to connect with potential clients. If your business is aimed at an international audience, for example, people from all over the world will potentially find you through your website. It is said that prospective customers will go onto a website for approximately seven seconds before making a decision. In that time, they are going to decide whether or not they want to connect with you further. So your website has to have *you* in there. Your prospective clients need to be able to feel your energy through your written word, dialogue and perhaps even video. If it is too formal and distant it is definitely not going to work, especially for an EFT business where you are going to be inviting your clients to open up to you. How can you expect them to do that when you are closed off in your first 'meeting' with them?

It is also important that you feel proud (as opposed to ashamed) of your website. This needs to be one place in business where you definitely don't make compromises. It is the part of your business and yourself that is out in the world. The website needs to have your heart, your soul and your message flowing through it, so you need to be happy with it.

> **EXERCISE:**
>
> If you already have your website built, go through it. Does it express your message? Does it have you in it? Does it reach out and connect with the kind of clients you would like to attract?

Some Key Elements of Your Website

So far, we have discussed the kind of impact that you want to be making with your website, but we haven't touched upon *how* to make that impact. The following guidelines will enable you to become more practical in building your presence.

The Homepage

The first place your prospective customers are likely to land is your homepage.

There are lots of different perspectives on what makes a good homepage. Some people say you should put your blog on your homepage. Although this can rank higher on Google, in my opinion, a blog on your homepage can be overwhelming for prospective clients (particularly those who are already overloaded with their emotional issues).

Opening with blogs doesn't create the connection that we are looking for, particularly as EFT practitioners. Instead, your first point of contact needs to be a place where you can express your message and connect with your clients, making them want to connect with you further. It needs to give them a taste of you and make them want to engage more. Think of your homepage as an advert. Keep it short and to the point. The worst kinds of homepages are the ones that contain six pages of information with everything that you could ever say about your business thrown at your prospective client. Have you ever gone to one of those websites and felt overwhelmed? That's the kind of effect we want to avoid for those who are looking to work with you. Think very simply, asking yourself "What is their need and how can I let them know that I am going to help them meet it?" Or "What is their problem and how can I show them that I am going to solve it with them?"

As a practitioner, you are probably already aware that people receive information in different ways. The main ways are audio, visual and kinaesthetic. Does your homepage enable people to receive the information in all three ways?

The 'Freebie' Offering

Remember, one of the main purposes of your website is to build your newsletter and list. You want to entice people to sign up for more information. If you are offering something for free when they sign up for your newsletter, you can keep regular communication with them through a blog or other offerings (such as free webinars). You might, for example, create a homepage with an arrow that says: "Claim your free video series here." It shows your clients exactly where to go, giving them a call to action that you direct them to. You need to direct your visitors.

Tools for Your Website

If you're multilingual, you can get a tool that translates your website into different languages. Don't use Google Translate for this purpose because, as I can tell you from personal experience when I used it, there were some curious translations that backfired at a later date!

Charging Online

If you want people to pay for your services online, PayPal integrates beautifully with websites, and offers a button facility so that people can see easily where to pay and have trust in the payment facility. If you are offering a shopping cart and selling programmes, books and so on, then you may want to use technology that is more sophisticated than Paypal, but for sessions and client programmes it is ideal.

Social Media Sharing

Ensure that you use social media sharing buttons on your site so that others can share your homepage, blogs and content easily. These are an important currency in today's social media-orientated market, and many referrals come this way, particularly if someone that a prospective client trusts shares your site with them.

'About Me' Page

This is the page where people get to connect with you. One of the biggest mistakes that people make on their About Me page is to list their credentials. Although your ego might not like it, your clients don't really care who you studied with and how many certificates you have. Your clients don't care so much about what you have done as they do about who you are. Your About Me page is where you get to share your story. Remember in Chapter 6 when we discussed the story behind your brand? This is very similar to what to write on your About Me page, and any work you did on writing the story behind your brand will go a long way to creating this page.

However, it isn't about sharing your whole life story. It's about skilfully identifying the key points of your story that your clients can relate to and that are relevant to what you are going to be helping them with. For example, I don't share too much information about my background as a dancer. However, you may remember that I touch upon the fact that when I was dancing at competition level, I learnt to push myself, and this was a challenge that I carried forward into creating my business. In that case, it is a relevant share.

Key points to include:

- Have a photo of yourself. Try to make sure it is relevant (a picture of you horse riding or skiing is probably not going to create the connection you require).
- Consider making a video (if you are comfortable in front of the camera). It is definitely a skill that requires practice — and tapping — for most of us!
- Explain why you do what you do. Make sure it contains emotions.
- Share your key life experiences (find a way to relate them to the work you are doing).
- Tell your prospective clients what your purpose is. People are more likely to invest in you if they know you are on fire with your purpose than if the work you are doing is a hobby.
- Share how you understand where the client is at this time.
- Talk about the transformation you experienced, how it has helped you, and what it has brought to your life.
- Reassure your prospective clients that you love to connect with people.
- Make sure there is a 'Contact Me' button at the end of the page — this is your call to action. *All the above is a waste if you don't give them a way to connect with you.*

BLOGS AND NEWSLETTERS

Both blogs and newsletters are written forms of communication that help to build your presence. A blog is a short, article-focused piece that's usually between four and six hundred words, going out on a regular basis. (However, blogs can be done in video form. Video blogs should be no more than four minutes long — 1½ to 3 minutes is ideal, as people will be more likely to instantly watch them; they won't be put off by a time commitment.) Either format enables you to keep in contact with your potential audience in a short written format that can go out weekly or monthly.

Your newsletter is a chance to share any forthcoming releases, events, special offers and so on with your clients. They usually go out monthly (at roughly the same time each month in order to build a steady presence).

In both your blog and your newsletter you can share a link to your website. In addition, both these forms of communication enable you to build yourself as an authority in your field (although a blog gives you more of an opportunity to create authority because you can talk about specific topics that you are knowledgeable about).

What to Blog About

Blog about something you can share uniquely.

If your specialism is working with phobias, for example, you could include some of the following in a series of blogs:

- Talk about where phobias come from
- Share some basic information on how tapping can help

- Share your own phobia experiences and why you chose this work
- Share case studies about others you have helped
- Talk about different topics each time such as flying, swimming, dogs, spiders and so on.

You can make your blogs as personal as you choose, remembering that a small amount of vulnerability over an issue you transformed can go a long way.

A good tip I got from Judith Morgan, creator of The Small Business Oracle, was to think about your blog as 'meat and two veg'. Create two gentle blogs and every third blog can give informative content that directly relates to gaining clients or selling products.

During a webinar I hosted with Kate Marillat, co-author of *Transform Your Beliefs, Transform Your Life*, we discussed a great way to think about the 'meat' of the content. Ask yourself, "What will my clients be googling at 2 am in the morning or when they are in a 'I have to sort this' state, looking for answers to help with their problem?" If the 'meat' blog is directed towards these Google searches, it will help your blog and its content reach your clients in their hour of need.

Rules for Blogging

- Keep it short—about 500 words is ideal, although sometimes this will vary depending on the topic.
- Use pictures — make it visually attractive. However, make sure your pictures are not copyrighted and you have the rights to use them. You can end up getting a £1,000 fine if

you use a picture that is copyrighted.

- Ask yourself, "Who is this blog for? What is this blog's purpose? What is the desired outcome of this particular blog?" each time you write.
- Keep it light and informative.
- Always have a biography section at the bottom of the blog so that people can find out about you, or have a call to action to connect with you.
- Always have your contact details visible so that people can connect to your email, website or phone number easily.

How Blogging Can Help To Build Your Business

You write a blog and share it in your newsletter, with your list, or on social media. You then ask your friends to share it with their friends. People read it, comment and sign up to your newsletter. You then start to create a community of people who enjoy reading your blogs. In the future, people will consider you a fountain of knowledge and contact you (this might not happen overnight!). When you launch client packages, special offers, workshops or products, you will have a list of people who are genuinely interested in your services.

TIPS ON NEWSLETTERS

Newsletters also enable you to share your courses, workshops, sessions and other offerings, giving people access to your business in a gentle way.

People want to hear about your success, so if you achieve something great, then let them know. Maybe you had an article published, created a product or passed an exam. You will inspire and empower 'your tribe' by being you.

Also, your newsletter is a great place to share other products, such as books or other people's services that you recommend. One tip — don't make your newsletter all about you; that way, your clients will see that you are gregarious in nature.

Make your newsletter visual. Keep the writing down to a minimum — it's best if you introduce the topic and then use a button that says, 'Learn more', which takes your clients to a page with all the information about that particular topic on it. Too much writing will switch your prospective clients off.

SOCIAL MEDIA – WHERE TO START

Social media is a great way to establish and build your presence. It allows you to connect with potential clients who are interested in what you do and want to learn from you.

Ensure that you keep it social. The best rule I've ever heard is: keep it 60% personal and 40% business, even on a business page. People want to connect with you because they want to know your thoughts and they want to know what's happening in your world.

It took me a long time before I would play on social media and when I did, I kept it extremely professional. However, the moment I started opening up and becoming 'me', people started to connect. As a result, there have been a lot of opportunities through Facebook that have generated business for me. I had an opportunity to go to New Zealand,

and that happened through Facebook. My workshop in San Francisco happened through Facebook too.

If you aren't familiar with using social media, pick one form to start with. If you try to do them all at once, you will spend too much time on them and spread yourself too thinly.

If you decide to work with multiple sites, ensure you know what the purpose for each one is. What do you want from LinkedIn? Why are you tweeting? And so on.

Dedicate time each day to be interactive and keep it consistent. Paul Zelizer created a massive online Facebook presence in his group Wisdompreneurs. He had thousands of active members within the first few months of launching, and his group continues to grow at a vast rate. When asked what the secret was, he said, "I created a steady, loving presence in the marketplace." He highlights how most new business owners are erratic with their presence, showing up repeatedly and then letting weeks or months go by before they communicate again. In order to build a presence that people trust, you need to show up intentionally and regularly.

Summary of Chapter Seven

a. **Presence is simply letting people know that your business exists.** When you develop your presence, your prospective clients are able to learn how your services and skill set could be of benefit to them.

b. **Your presence needs to invite your potential clients to have a dialogue with you.** In the old paradigm of business, presence used to be about "Here I am and this is what I do!" The new paradigm is more akin to "Here we both are, this is what I do, how can it be of service to you and your challenges?"

c. **Maintaining regular, authentic contact with your potential clients boosts their confidence in you.** The key to building presence is consistency, which helps your clients build trust in you. It reinforces your name and services in their awareness and even if they don't require your services at this time, they will be able to recall your name or service to their friends because of the trust they have built in you.

Ways to create presence include:

- Websites
- Blogs
- Newsletters
- Teleclasses / webinars
- Flyers
- Interviews
- Press releases
- Magazine articles
- Presentations / talks
- Podcasts
- Social Media profiles

Chapter

Marketing

How does the word 'marketing' make you feel?

If your answer is anything other than light or joyful then before you even begin marketing, you need to change your relationship to how you feel about it. If you are fearful, apprehensive and hesitant about marketing, that will show up in the way you put yourself across in business.

Marketing isn't something you can choose to opt out of. To have a successful practice, you've got to be able to market yourself. When I talk about marketing, I simply mean letting people know what you do and how it can help the challenges that they have. The problem is, we often get this mixed it up in our heads with advertising, which is usually manipulating people into buying things by triggering their fears and insecurities.

Google's definition of marketing is: "The action or business of promoting and selling products or services, including market research and advertising."

What this means is that marketing is just the means and ways of sharing your passion, gifts and purpose with the world. It's just a process. If the thought of that process brings up some underlying issues, that means that you may have some work to do. So, in this chapter we'll help you change your relationship to marketing so you can confidently share the presence we started to build in the last chapter with the wider world.

MARKETING AND EMOTIONS

If marketing is just a process, why does it bring up so many issues for us? The truth is, it isn't usually marketing that triggers us, but the thought of putting ourselves out there. Two of the most frequent responses when I get to the bottom of this with clients are: "Perhaps they won't like me," and "Maybe I don't know enough." Some people have even told me that they are quite happy being invisible, but underlying this message is usually a subtler truth: "I don't want to be seen because I am quite happy playing small or remaining in the background." It can feel safer to hide behind not marketing ourselves than it can to stand up and be counted for what we do.

Some of the students on my business programme expressed the fear, "But what if I get it wrong?" Putting ourselves out there in this way can open us up to all kinds of self-judgements.

There can also be a sense of vulnerability and apprehension that sceptics might attack. Being an EFT practitioner requires some bravery. We know that our technique can look anywhere from slightly strange to totally ridiculous to an outsider. It's easy to hide behind this fear and not feel brave enough to stand by something that looks dubious to the untrained eye.

> **REFLECTION POINT:**
>
> Are you worried about others judging you for what you put out into the world? If so, why? Is it really judgement about you or is it about their beliefs and perceptions? Can you recognise that in many cases, those who would be judging you are actually the people who will benefit the most from you? How does your perception shift when you own that your message will resonate with the people you are meant to serve?

On the other end of the scale, we can find ourselves fearing an overwhelming amount of success. We know we have a tool that creates great results. Will we be able to cope if we excel at what we do and we start getting lots of attention for helping others? It might seem like an odd question, but if you have been used to hanging back out of the limelight, success can feel very scary and unwelcoming.

> **MARKETING EXERCISE:**
>
> Write down your response to the following question: "How does marketing make me feel?"

The following are some of the responses we received from practitioners like yourself on the *Realise Your Magical Business Internet Program:*

- "I don't know how to…"
- "I just go blank."
- "It makes me panic because EFT is very new and not necessarily straightforward to market."
- "The thought of selling myself makes my body constrict and tighten up."
- "Marketing makes me feel very analytical. My focus becomes: How many people signed up or bought my service and not the joy of sharing what I am passionate about."
- "Marketing to unknown people terrifies me and makes me feel exhausted. It's pointless and a waste of time. It's expensive. What the hell do I say anyway?"
- "I feel confused about where to begin or what to do. I don't have very much money to spend on marketing. It makes me feel very apprehensive—like even the word 'marketing' is scary and I just want to put it off to sometime later down the road."
- "Sometimes I feel like I am not big enough yet to need marketing."

You may be able to relate to some or all of the above responses. You will probably also recognise that if you are feeling this way you will not be productive, passionate or purposeful when introducing yourself to potential clients.

> ### EXERCISE:
>
> We often have many judgements about marketing, and about people who market, that all come from our belief systems.
>
> What judgements do you have? And who did you learn them from?
>
> Break them down into memories and tap on them.

I had a conversation with a friend of mine, Natasha Black, who had an interesting take on the importance of us sharing our gifts to the world. She believes it is a crime to not put ourselves out there and let people know what we do. We are not serving ourselves or the people we could potentially empower. Hopefully you will admit that this is worse than overcoming the word 'marketing'?

We go into this business because we want to give service and we want to help people. We realise that we have fantastic tools and techniques that allow us to do that, combined with the knowledge that we have gained along the way. In EFT, the biggest catchphrase is "*EFT works where nothing else will.*" We have a miraculous tool, literally at our fingertips, and we want to be able to share it.

> **REFLECTION POINT:**
>
> Take a step back from marketing and consider how fantastic it is that we can be a part of helping people to transform their lives. And then remind yourself that not sharing will not only mean that you are not living your purpose, but that you are restricting them from living theirs too.
>
> If this brings you into overwhelm, then definitely tap until you find the underlying belief.

A SHIFT IN PERSPECTIVE

Sometimes changing the way we feel about marketing requires simply a shift in perspective. If marketing were actually called "sharing your gifts, sharing your passion and sharing your magic," how would it feel to you? Would it still bring up the same emotions?

Which joyful phrase would you use to describe sharing your gifts with the world instead of 'marketing'?

Sometimes when we rephrase it, we literally strip away some of the emotion.

> **EXERCISE:**
>
> Pick one form of marketing that you would like to develop in your business.
>
> Identify three action steps that you can take with that one form over the next two to three weeks.
>
> Commit to those action steps by announcing them to a friend or make a note to yourself in writing.

The reason I encourage you to write your action steps down is that the quality changes when you commit them to paper. You tell the universe that this is what you are doing. When you share your plans with others, you also create accountability.

> **EXERCISE: MARKETING RESEARCH ACTIVITY**
>
> One of the ways of becoming a better marketer is to begin researching other people's websites so you start to spot the most effective strategies that others are using.
>
> Start by researching other practitioner's websites — both those who practice different modalities and

those who offer similar services to yours. Try and do this from the perspective of a client, putting yourself in their shoes. What do you like? Are there any things that are consistently a turn-off for you?

Check out their About Me page. Notice how you feel when they share vulnerably from the heart as opposed to when they list their qualifications. Which ones do you feel you trust the most?

Notice the ones that are sharing how they can help their clients. Contrast this to the ones that describe their technique. Again, where do you feel most drawn?

Also check out their sign-up processes, designs and layouts, booking and paying systems and start piecing together what is most effective.

By the end of this exercise, you should have more of an idea of how you want your website to look and also how you want your prospective clients to feel when they arrive there. Don't underestimate the importance of this exercise. The more you understand your world, the more effective you will be at becoming a viable player in your field.

Carry out a similar exercise for social media pages, newsletters, blog posts and so on.

VIDEO

If you are thinking of creating videos on your website, consider the kind of videos you would enjoy creating.

• Case studies

- Informative
- Testimonials
- Creative
- Interviews

Remember, marketing is you making yourself visible for people to find you. How you make yourself visible is up to you. If videos appeal to you, make sure you make them from a place that is joyful to you. Pretty much everyone that starts out making a video needs to get over the initial discomfort about being on camera. Once you have got over that (it takes some people months to do so), ensure that the whole process is enjoyable. You aren't obligated to make videos but it is a very effective way for your potential clients to connect with you.

IDENTIFY PEAK TIMES PEOPLE WILL LOOK FOR YOU

In every business there are busy times and quieter times, and even the most successful business has peaks and troughs. When you experience a quiet time, instead of going into a panic that nobody is ever going to come again, use it to get your promotional material ready ahead of the busier periods.

If you have a specialism, you may see peaks during the following periods:

Weight Loss
Before or after Christmas, before or after holidays

Addictions
New Year's, after the summer

Parenting
Spring, Autumn, a few months after a big sporting event such as the Football World Cup

Trauma
New Year's, or holidays such as Christmas and Thanksgiving; anniversaries of traumatic events or big news stories

Goals
New Year's, holidays such as Christmas and Thanksgiving, September or after the summer holidays

Remember that times of year will impact your promotion and business. There is little point in trying to promote goals and weight loss throughout the summer; however, towards the end of August into September is a great time. Be conscious of the news and what is happening, as this could give you a chance to boost your promotion through blog writing, radio interviews, and teleseminars. When people are thinking about a certain issue, they will be more open to respond.

When you know this, you can be easier about having quieter times in your business. It means you replace that less productive thought of: "Perhaps nobody will ever come again," with the more solution-focused thought of: "How can I use this time to attract more clients at a later date?"

Remember, marketing is simply understanding the needs and requirements of your potential clients and letting them know how you can help. It is also understanding and identifying what your customers really want (and when they want it).

EXERCISE:

Identify when your clients may be looking for your services. When are the times they are most likely to be picking up a phone or inquiring about sessions or workshops?

Your Call To Action

A reminder that the whole message that sits at the centre of your marketing material—be it your website, blogs, newsletters, or videos—needs to be geared towards one primary outcome. That is, knowing what your clients want and showing them that you know what they want. When they are looking at the material, they should easily be able to answer the question: "What's in it for me?"

Your message should consistently emphasise that you understand your prospective customer and you know what they are going through. This is the secret of how to resonate with your clients. They need to feel supported and understood before they even connect with you.

However, once you have established what your client wants, it's important not to stop there. You need to give them a call to action that directs them to contact you.

A call to action might sound like a very formal term, but it is really what you want your clients to do once they have connected to you through your marketing. It is how you turn yourself into someone that can help them, rather than someone that simply understands them.

Imagine this scenario. You are on a bus going through a city that you don't know. You suddenly realise that you are lost. You turn to the nearest person. They sympathise with you and share a time when they were lost too. You don't feel so alone anymore. But nothing changes. You are still lost. Now imagine the same scenario but with a different outcome. You tell the person sitting next to you that you are lost. Immediately they give you guidance on how to get to where you need to go. Not only do you feel met and understood, but you also have a solution to your challenge. The same scenario is true for your marketing material. You don't just want to be the person that can empathise with other people's challenges. You want to be the one that can help them with solutions. In order to do that, you need to direct them to contact you so that you can offer them solutions.

Remember, your clients are coming to you for guidance, mentorship and help. If they didn't need those things they wouldn't be reaching out to you. And your marketing needs to be clear about how you are going to give that help.

In practical terms, you need to decide if your call to action means that you want them to pick up the phone and call you, or email you, or book a 20-minute, no obligation, consultation with you. Because at the end of your marketing, you need to direct them to do that.

EXERCISE: YOUR CALL TO ACTION

First, get clear on what kinds of clients you want. Are you looking for your clients for sessions, workshops, group telecalls, teleseminars, webinars?

> Would you like the one-to-one clients; are you happy working on Skype, have you been working face-to-face?
>
> Decide your preferred call to action. Is it client phone calls, emailing inquiries, having them sign up to a newsletter, having them book on your course, etc.?
>
> Begin to build your call to action into your marketing.

More on Offering a 20-Minute Consultation

If you decide to offer a consultation, your marketing might be summarised into something along these lines: "OK, so you have this problem and I know what that means; you are probably feeling like this and this; and would you like to chat about it for 20 minutes so I can share how I can help you?" You might add, "Booking a 20-minute consultation with me is absolutely free and with no obligation. It's so we can both check if we are a match to working together."

A call to action such as this means that you also get to decide if the client is the right match for you. This means that you avoid the trap of people signing up expecting one-hit wonders. You might be able to work with people who have a phobia in one or two sessions and get results, but if you work with more complex challenges such as severe trauma or serious disease, talking to the client for twenty minutes will enable them to see that a more long-term intervention is needed. If you offer packages, this is also a good opportunity to see if the client is willing to commit to more sessions at a reduced rate (we'll discuss this further when we come to Chapter 10 on money).

GAINING TESTIMONIALS

Testimonials give new and potential clients trust, confidence and insight into results you've already achieved from happy customers.

Traditionally, testimonials were in written form, sometimes with the person's initials and location and other times with the full name and a photograph (with the written permission of the client).

Video testimonials have become more popular, but unless clients offer to do a video testimonial, it is preferable to ask them for a written one. Make sure you ask whether you can use their real name or not.

Workshop or course attendees are usually happy to give a video testimonial at the end if they have enjoyed the course.

The Importance of Asking

You very rarely get testimonials without asking! Don't wait for people to offer, as they are generally focused on their experience and not on promoting your business for you.

It can be daunting to ask when you first start out, but if your client has great results, it is obviously very helpful if they are willing to share their experience, particularly at the end of working with you. Most people don't object, especially if their anonymity and session confidentiality are respected.

Even if you aren't seeing clients yet, you can obtain testimonials from swap partners and case studies.

> **EXERCISE: ASKING FOR TESTIMONIALS**
>
> Do you feel fear about asking for testimonials? Tune into that feeling.
>
> What is the emotion? Does it have a colour and shape? What is its purpose for being there? What is the belief behind it? (For example: not worthy, not good enough, etc.)
>
> Tap on it!

Summary of Chapter Eight

a.   **Before you even begin marketing, you need to change your relationship to how you feel about it.** A negative relationship to the word 'marketing' will affect your willingness to actually do it!

b.   **Marketing isn't something you can choose to opt out of.** To have a successful practice, you've got to be able to market yourself.

c.   **Marketing is just the means and ways of sharing your passion, gifts and purpose with the world.** It's just a process.

d.   **Sometimes changing the way we feel about marketing requires simply a shift in perspective.** If marketing were actually called "sharing your gifts, sharing your passion and sharing your magic," it might not have the same impact upon you.

e.   **Identify the peak times that people will be looking for you.** Create your marketing around those times.

f.   **Ensure your marketing has a call to action.** It needs to direct your clients to reach out to you.

g.   **Ask for testimonials from satisfied clients.** It's a great way of building new customers' trust in you.

Chapter

9

Client Attraction

Who is your ideal client?

Often when I ask this question of practitioners, I am met with a seemingly humble answer. "I am in service, and I work with anyone who comes to me with a problem." However, while this might seem noble, this kind of response brings several challenges. Firstly, it assumes that as practitioners we do not get to choose who our clients are. This takes us back to the old paradigm of being self-sacrificing that we touched upon in the earlier chapters of this book. Secondly, if we aren't clear who we serve, then how can we let the universe know that we are here for them? It is very challenging to attract clients if we don't know who it is we are manifesting.

When you know who you are serving you can connect your marketing to them more efficiently. Your prospective clients have a collective belief system, and a similar drive to work with you. When you understand that, you can deeply connect to them with your message.

When I think of my ideal clients, I know they have to have some kind of drive to achieve their goal. I'm best serving those who are already motivated, as opposed to those who don't have a spark to achieve. My ideal clients know what they want. They might not know how to get it; they may feel like it's an impossible task, but they know in their hearts what it is they want and they are willing to try.

> **REFLECTION POINT:**
>
> What kinds of qualities do you look for in your clients? List the personal qualities that you want your clients to have, so that you get clear on who you are best matched to work with.

When you know what personal qualities you wish your clients to have, what you are really asking for is people who you can be in rapport with. It's easy to fake or simulate rapport. There are many exercises that teach us how to build rapport through the use of techniques. But for me, true rapport is naturally there with the people we most click or connect with in life. Surely those are the people that you would like to serve too — the ones you feel that special something with. Then the sessions take on their own fire and magic; you don't feel like you are swimming upstream. Deciding the qualities you are looking for in clients before you attract them means that you can then tailor your marketing to speak directly to these people. You are offering a kinder service because you are letting prospective clients know upfront the kinds of people you are best matched to help.

Why Clients Come To You

In Chapter 6 we highlighted why particular clients would

be coming to you. (If you don't remember why, we will recap shortly.) Keep reminding yourself until it is set in your bones. Because why people come to you is part of the heartbeat of your business.

Are they blocked, are they wanting more from life? Are they going to be looking for practical and emotional support? The following exercise will help remind you.

> **RECAP EXERCISE:**
>
> What are the five reasons why your potential clients may choose the tools and techniques that you use?
>
> What are the top five benefits your clients get from these techniques?
>
> What would be the top five benefits of working with you specifically?

Consistently reminding yourself of why people are coming to you will help you to manifest more clients because you are tuning into the needs of those you are here to help.

THERE'S NO COMPETITION

While we are on the subject of client attraction, it is easy to assume that we need to compete with others who are serving a similar client base. That kind of thinking comes from scarcity consciousness, and feeling we are in competition with other practitioners will directly affect client attraction. We can get triggered into thoughts such as "Other practitioners are better than me," or "Their marketing is more powerful than mine," or "There aren't enough clients to go around."

When you think of how many billions of people there are in the world and consider that you are looking for somewhere between six and twenty clients a week, there are definitely more than enough clients for everyone. The key is that when you get really clear about who you are serving, then you can ensure your message reaches the right group of people. You are going to be a match for one person and another practitioner is not, and vice versa. Knowing who it is you are best matched to helping is a big part of attracting the right people to you.

EXERCISE:

Have you been comparing yourself to other practitioners? If so, tap on the underlying belief systems that are keeping you caught in the competitive mindset.

What's The Best Way for You to Connect With Your Clients?

Now you have a better idea of who you are serving and have begun to move to the mindset that there are plenty of clients to go around, the next step is to work out how to reach them. One of the best ways to find out how to reach clients who you can be in rapport with is to consider how *you* like to hear about the services that others are offering. Is it through email? Is it an informal chat over the telephone? Is it through talks or groups?

When people send me too many sales-type emails I switch off almost immediately. I'd much rather connect with someone over the telephone. I'd also much rather receive a flyer through my postbox than a marketing email. I'm also a fan of Facebook and blogs.

When you understand how you like to receive information, you can have more ease promoting to potential clients. It will feel more authentic and less 'markety' to you.

> **EXERCISE:**
>
> Identify your top three ways of receiving information. Are these the methods you have been using to reach out to clients so far? If not, what needs to adjust in your business so you are using methods that are authentically aligned with you?

WHERE CAN YOU FIND YOUR POTENTIAL CLIENTS?

So now you know your preferred method of communication, how are you going to reach clients? If you are working locally or looking to set up groups or workshops, then you need to be proactive in the community you are choosing to work with. The key is to put a face to the message you are sharing and let people know you are available to help them.

If people are looking for help for a particular issue such as weight loss, chances are they will have tried many things before EFT.

They may been to the doctor's, weight loss groups, diet groups, health food shops, fitness groups, exercise classes and gyms. Making yourself known to these places and setting up an introduction enables you to get your name out there. Not all of them will be receptive (and you will have to prepare yourself for some nos). However, a reputation is built by consistently showing up and owning what you do. You may not see results overnight, but you will start to build a name for yourself.

If you are working online, a good way to build your reputation is on forums and other online discussion groups. Find groups which already have your potential clients within them. Don't advertise yourself directly, but rather go in and give advice on your particular topic, helping others to solve problems. Many people build a business through showing up on Facebook and advising others for free. It builds trust and rapport so that clients can reach out to you.

If you are starting to build your list, then teleclasses, webinars, conference calls and Google Hangout chats are a great way for people to connect with you before they commit to working with you.

HOW DO YOU FEEL ABOUT PUTTING YOURSELF OUT THERE?

So far in this chapter we have been very practical. You have some strategies to enable you to connect with the clients that you are here to serve. However, we definitely don't want to ignore the fact that not knowing what to do practically may have been masking an even deeper issue: your fear of stepping out.

Attracting new clients usually comes with a multitude of emotions. These include vulnerability, overwhelm, and when they are not showing up, despair. "Where are they? Can I do this? What am I doing?" are familiar thoughts that may go through your head as you start to put yourself out there more.

EXERCISE:

What emotions does expanding your client base bring up for you?
- Fear?
- Vulnerability?
- Overwhelm?
- Despair?
- Worry?
- Other?

And when you tune in to that emotion, what beliefs are underpinning it? Perhaps...
- I'll be rejected
- I'm invisible
- I'm not good enough
- Why would people come to me
- I can't charge for what I do
- They won't understand tapping or what I do.

Whatever you are faced with, keep tapping, because if you are simultaneously drawing clients towards you and energetically pushing them away, it is going to create a division in you that won't be good for business.

When I first started out, I thought that as soon as people heard the amazing stories that I was sharing they would book in for consultations. When they didn't, I went into freeze mode. "I know how to market. They're just not coming, what's wrong?" I instantly turned it inwards on myself, "Will they ever come? What's wrong with me?" Behind these thoughts were hurt, anger and frustration which all led to beliefs about me not being good enough and not loveable. I had to do some deep self-work before I was ready to work with others. Starting a business can definitely be considered a self-growth path all on its own. It highlights our unresolved issues in a very unique and confronting way.

This 'not good enough' belief didn't resolve overnight for me. It even carried into my work as a trainer. The challenge I had was that EFT Master Karl Dawson, who had not only trained me and helped me heal but had also created Matrix Reimprinting, ran EFT courses forty minutes away from me.

In my own mind I was sabotaging myself because at the time I didn't value myself enough to believe that people would want to come and learn from me. As a result, I frequently had to cancel my courses and I often recommended people to Karl's courses. However, I had one course attendee who changed that for me. After telling her my course was cancelled (again) and suggesting she go to train with Karl, she highlighted how she had connected with my story and was very keen to train with me. I hadn't seen it that way until then, but it was a real turning point in understanding that people choose to work with people for very personal reasons and it is much more about resonance than anything else.

The connection that you make with others will attract them into your business. That's why they will come to you. Clearing your blocks will enable you to get out of your own way so you can truly show up for those connections with your clients and benefit their lives with your passion and purpose.

Exercise for Client Attraction

If money weren't an issue, how many clients would you

want to be bringing in? How many new clients would you want to be generating each week or each month?

In order to enable these clients to come in, we need to create an energetic space for them. One of the tricks that I frequently teach my clients is to double the energy of that which they would like to create. Often when people say they want ten clients (and consistently work on this on an energetic level), they actually get eight or nine. It's as if we decide what is just enough and focus our energy on that.

However, as energy constantly moves and expands, we want to ride that wave, rather than the wave of limitation, or having just enough. Ensuring that you are energetically open for approximately double of what you want is a great way to keep expanding and to keep yourself out of limitation and lack. This exercise was adapted from an exercise by a friend of mine, Michelle Kania.

EXERCISE: DOUBLE IT

Whatever number of clients (or workshop participants) you would like, close your eyes, tap on your finger points, take a few deep breaths and focus on that number.

Notice how the number of people that you have decided on feels to you energetically. If there's any fear, tap until you feel comfortable. If any strong beliefs or memories come up, pause the exercise and deal with them, before you return to it.

Once you are comfortable with your original number, expand your original number by two. Add two more people and allow the energy to settle, opening up to receiving two more people, per week, per month, or whatever you chose. Keep tapping until that energy feels comfortable within your body.

It should feel like these clients are coming to you with ease and joy and that it's easy to make space and time for them.

Once you are comfortable, expand it again by another five. Allow that energy to settle and become the norm, to be part of your business and who you are. Then, bring in more people until you have doubled the amount that you originally set, gently expanding, receiving, opening to sharing your gifts and your services with more and more people.

See your diary filled with appointments or workshops filled with people.

Notice the colour, the positive feelings and the emotions that are attached to this expansion. Tune into the positive emotions you feel from the new number. Then, borrowing the reimprinting process from Matrix Reimprinting, take the new picture with its positive emotions and colour in through the top of your head, let it move around your body and through your cells, take it into your heart, and then use your heart to send the picture out into the universe in every direction, rewriting the old picture with the new information.

Practice the above exercise regularly until you are comfortable with expanding beyond your current limitations.

JUDGING YOUR CLIENTS

There is one more vital piece to client attraction, and that is how much you accept or judge your potential clients. It's tricky to admit and face, but it is definitely something that needs addressing. Because the truth is, the extent to which we still judge ourselves will show up in any judgements we have about where our clients are on their path. This will also affect our relationship with them and how we attract them.

Sometimes we do this to the detriment of our business. Have you ever been contacted by a client and believed that they couldn't afford your services before they had clearly stated whether they could or not? This is a destructive form of judgement that stands in the way of you gaining a new client.

I used to keep myself small or hesitant when people asked my prices: I was so worried about them and their finances that I couldn't focus on the benefits I could bring. As a result, I would attract clients who wanted EFT to work quickly, in a session or two. Then more judgement came in, because I started judging my clients for wanting EFT to work quickly!

Other judgements include things such as "They aren't spiritual enough," or "They won't understand tapping," and so on. Sometimes we don't even know we are making these judgements, but whether it's conscious or not, our potential clients may sense that something is off.

When we place judgements on our clients, we are entering a relationship based on a projection of who they are. As soon as we do that, we don't really hear them.

In contrast, if we can meet them from an open place, without judgements or projections, beyond our own beliefs and filters, we can really start to hear them.

> **OBSERVATION:**
>
> Be aware when you are talking to people about what you do. What mind chatter is going on in your head about what they may be thinking? What are you thinking — about what they may be thinking?!

I had an interesting experience when I was running the belief "They can't afford it." A prospective client rang me up and said, "I'm really interested in working with you. At the moment I am not working." I instantly heard myself silently saying, "He can't afford it." What he was actually saying to me was: "I don't have that job and I don't have family commitments so I can give it everything that I've got to working together right now." We started working together daily. However, because I was running my belief that he couldn't afford it, I offered him half-price sessions.

Within three sessions, he told me he was a multi-millionaire! I realised the disservice I had done to myself and also to him. I hadn't given him the chance to invest in me for what I was worth. (We'll discuss this concept further when we come to Chapter 10 on money.) In addition, I hadn't valued myself either, and was inconsistent in my pricing as a result.

This is why it is important to look at our judgements and perceptions so that we can remain open and constantly curious about what is possible.

Another judgement we can run is "EFT doesn't work quickly enough." When we do our EFT training, we all learn about the many "one-minute wonders" that EFT produces. However, most of our clients that come to see us haven't been on those trainings, they don't know about those "one-minute wonders" and they don't know what you know about EFT.

Perhaps they go out the door feeling better, but you're beating yourself up because you haven't got them from a 10 down to a 0. They may have shifted from a 10 to a 7 or a 6 and be feeling on top of the world because of those results, but you are too busy judging the session because it didn't go at the pace you were expecting or hoping. You project the results you want, and even though the client may be happy with their shift (and the fact that it could be the first time in years that they made any progress with this problem), you feel as though something has failed somewhere.

There can also be a feeling that it's our responsibility to heal our clients. However, as soon as we take the responsibility away from them, we are disempowering them.

When you are building your message, and you don't have all these judgements and perceptions about what your clients *may* be thinking or feeling, they can really start to hear you and what you are offering. But more importantly, your clients feel like you are more in rapport with them. A big part of client attraction is moving beyond any preconceived idea of the results that your prospective clients may have, and instead showing up with curiosity to see what you can shift together. When you do this, you will be of far greater service to your client than when you are trying to second-guess all the time, and putting a barrier between you as a result.

Summary of Chapter Nine

a. **You need to know who you want to serve so that you can let the universe know that you are here for them.** When you know who you are serving you can connect your marketing to them more efficiently.

b. **When you know what personal qualities you wish your clients to have, what you are really asking for is people with whom you can have rapport.** Deciding the qualities you are looking for in clients before you attract them means that you can then tailor your marketing to speak directly to these people.

c. **It is easy to assume that we need to compete with others who are serving a similar client base.** You will be a match for certain people and not others. The key is that when you get really clear about who you are serving, then you can ensure your message reaches the right group of people.

d. **Clarifying the way that *you* like to receive information will enable you to market authentically to your prospective clients.** It will mean that you can share your message in a way that feels in alignment with you.

e. **In order to enable clients to come in, we need to create an energetic space for them.** One of the tricks that I frequently teach my clients is to double the energy of that which they would like to create.

f. **Ensure you are not judging your clients and blocking yourself from receiving from them as a result.** When you are building your message, and you don't have judgements and perceptions about what your clients *may* be thinking or feeling, they can really start to hear you and what you are offering.

Chapter

70

Money

Money was born from an exchange system. Originally, it went something like this: "You've got potatoes. I've got sheep. Want to swap?"

Eventually we started operating in a currency system. It started in China with cowry shells. In 500 BC, the Turks used pieces of silver, which the Greeks and Persians improved upon. When the Romans actually created a Protectress of Funds, money started to be stored and, with the expansion of the Roman Empire, it became something to be revered.

However, we have lost sight of the fact that money was originally an exchange system. We have put too much value, including our self-worth, on this exchange system. We learn beliefs that money is bad or the root of all evil. Then we feel conflicted about earning a living.

Consider this in a different way. Think about the amount of emotions we load onto money as a result of our conditioning and programming. If somebody were dumping that amount of emotion on you, would you want to be there for them? Would you want to help them? When you start to think about money as an energy exchange you can start to see more clearly how you are relating to it.

MONEY JUDGEMENTS AND BELIEFS

When we have judgements and conclusions about how we expect our relationship with money to be, we block our receiving. Our energy contracts as a result, and we can't see or manifest solutions. Once we come to a conclusion about how something will be, it stops the energy flowing.

How many times have you decided beforehand about how money is going to come to you? As soon as you have an entrenched belief, or make a judgement or conclusion, you will notice that your energy becomes blocked.

Long ago when I worked in recruitment, I went through a sales training with a phenomenal mentor called Frank Swain. One of the first things he taught me was that when you want to create more possibility, you need to ask open-ended questions. When you ask closed questions you only allow yes or no answers. By asking closed questions you instantly shut down any chance of conversation or knowledge gathering. Open-ended questions typically start with 'How' and 'Why'. By asking open-ended questions, you allow for the answers to come from all the places you have never thought of.

In EFT, we use open-ended questions when we ask, "How does that make you feel?" In contrast, if we ask our clients, "Does that make you feel bad?", we aren't leaving the space for all possibilities, and instead are projecting from the limitations of our own experience.

The same applies with manifestation. We often need to know more information, create dialogue and an openness to receive outside the limitations of our perception or experience.

Later in life I discovered a tool called Access Consciousness which proposes a similar question that you can ask in any situation. The question is: "How is it possible to/that ...?"

However, most of us don't ask this question in relation to manifesting money. Most of us say something along the lines of "I'm only going to receive money from clients," or "I'm only going to receive money from workshops," or "I'm only going to receive money from my job." When we continuously make conclusions about the source of our money, we don't leave energetic space for other money to come to us. In Chapter 11 we are going to discuss business planning and, while it is good practice to name the number of clients you want, if you don't leave space for growth in directions outside of those that you can currently imagine, you limit your business.

Money can come in various different forms: from tax rebates to wins on lottery tickets, to inheritance from people that we didn't even know we were related to. It can also come from someone approaching you about a project or opportunity that you hadn't even thought of. By keeping ourselves open to receiving by (as they say in Access Consciousness) "living in the question", we open ourselves to possibilities.

When it comes to money, we often use it to limit our possibilities. Have you ever thought, "No, I can't do that. It's too expensive," or "No, that's never going to happen," or "That dream's going to have to wait." When you make a conclusion like this you are putting the condition of money on it; whereas when you understand that money is energy and the universe is energy, opportunities can come from a range of unexpected directions.

This kind of approach also requires trust and patience. Sometimes we expect the change to happen overnight. Perhaps new seeds are just beginning to sprout but the mind jumps in, judges that the progress is not fast enough, and closes the energy off again. The outcome is that you end up building an erratic relationship with money, which continues to be inconsistent and unpredictable in nature.

Your Money as Your Lover

If your money were your lover, what would you be saying to him or her?

This question, which also originated from Access Consciousness, is a dynamic way of enabling us to examine our relationship with money.

> **EXERCISE:**
> **PART ONE: MONEY AS YOUR LOVER**
>
> Imagine money being your husband, wife, partner or lover. What would they look like? What would they feel like? How would you be reacting with them?
>
> When you look at your relationship with them, what do you think? Is it a healthy partnership or are you heading for divorce? Are there positives? Are there negatives?
>
> Take a moment to focus on the negatives. If that person were in front of you, what negative things would you be saying to them or thinking about them?
>
> Would you be saying: "I don't trust you, I've given up so much just to have you. You're never there for me. Where are you? Where have you been?"
>
> Maybe there is anger there. Are you saying, "I can't forgive you. You really don't make me happy. Why are you cheating on me with the bills," and so on.
>
> Or perhaps there is no communication and you can barely picture the relationship.

When we carry out this exercise we can begin to understand how we treat those pieces of paper that trigger so much of our conditioning and programming. When you know that money is about exchange, you can start to clear some of the rubble of the old relationship and build a new one, based on flowing energy rather than stagnant beliefs.

Imagine, for example, that your lover was saying to you, "I can't rely on you!" or "My happiness depends on you."

What kind of relationship would that create? How much pressure would you feel? It's the same kind of pressure that we put on those pieces of paper that we call money.

EXERCISE:
PART TWO: TAPPING ON YOUR MONEY AS YOUR LOVER

Now that you have identified your money's love identity, begin tapping.

What emotions come to you as you picture your money as a lover?

Tap through any strong, negative emotions until they reduce to less than a 3.

You might experience anger, resentment, hurt, sadness and abandonment. Keep tapping through the emotional layers.

When you feel calmer and less reactive, close your eyes and imagine an image of your money as your lover. Step into the picture, still tapping, and meet them.

Talk to this new money 'partner'. Take the time to say what you need to say. If you want to ask for forgiveness, say it. Ask or say what you need to say to your partner.

Also allow that partner to respond to you. Listen to them. Hear what they have to say. How does your partner feel emotionally?

If need be, tap on your money partner and release any negative emotion that comes up for them.

Remember that their emotion is valid and if you find you are triggered into defence, tap on yourself in this picture.

What needs to happen in order for you two to work together in a partnership?

Which colour represents the beginning of this new relationship? Surround both of you with that colour.

What's the next step in your relationship? Would you be willing to make the commitment to take that next step?

Agree that you will come back regularly to discuss how things are going and to build more on your new connection.

When the picture is a positive one, borrowing some elements from Matrix Reimprinting, take it in through the top of your head, allowing all the neurons in your brain to reconnect with the new beliefs and emotions you have around this new relationship. Send the information through your cells before taking it into your heart. Use your heart to send the new information out into the universe, rewriting your old money patterns as you do.

Go back to this image after a few days, checking in with your partner. See how the relationship has grown since you started listening to one another. Keep tapping as you support and nurture the relationship. Continue to have this meeting at a set time just as you are doing with the business identity exercise. Make sure you schedule the time.

COMFORT ZONES

"Of course it's going to be uncomfortable to get out of your comfort zone, because if you're not in a comfort zone it's going to be uncomfortable."

Brett Moran

A comfort zone is a place where you feel safe or at ease without stress. It is like the safety blanket of a small child. When you've got situations that occur over and over again with your money, such as getting into debt in familiar ways or going overdrawn and getting charged, it's usually because there's a comfort zone to the old pattern for you. That comfort zone has obviously been created from your belief systems.

Emotionally and energetically, it is easier to stay with what we know financially than 'rocking the boat' and enabling change so that we can have all that we have dreamed about.

EXERCISE: YOUR COMFORT ZONE

Imagine your comfort zone. What picture comes to mind when you think about it? Now imagine your discomfort zone. What picture comes to mind for it? What emotions are associated with each?

Starting with your discomfort zone, tap on the emotions and feelings attached to the picture.

How does the picture change when you do? Is it less uncomfortable? Now look at your original comfort picture. Has anything changed now you have tapped on the discomfort picture?

My personal example:

My comfort zone was represented by a warm picture of being snuggled in a chair with a blanket in front of a log fire. My discomfort zone was in a mountainous area, where it was dark, raining and cold. I was hiking alone in the second picture. After tapping on how the discomfort zone picture made me feel ("Even though I have this dark, cold picture that makes me feel overwhelmed and sad, I love and accept myself..."), the picture started to transform into a sunny and open area that I was happy to play in. So both my comfort zone and discomfort zone became attractive. My need to retreat was fulfilled and my need to discover, play and have adventures in new areas was fulfilled too.

It's not just asking for money that can be a challenge. It is also being ready to receive it. The following exercise will enable you to open up to receiving more.

EXERCISE:

If you suddenly receive money, how are your friends going to react to you? How's your family going to react? What would it mean about you?
What are the benefits to having more money?
What are the problems to having more money?
What part of you will you have to give up in order to have more money?
Which negative belief or emotion is your current financial situation serving?

Your answers will enable you to see where you are either blocking yourself from receiving money or remaining in your comfort zone due to your conditioning. Tap on any judgements that you perceive others will make about you for moving out of your comfort zone.

ASKING FOR MONEY FROM CLIENTS

When you think about asking for money, what happens in your body?

Do you get the sense that it doesn't matter either way? Perhaps you start off really well and then experience mind chatter when it comes to stating your prices. Or maybe you limit yourself by not charging what you are worth.

So when you're asking for money, do you find it comfortable to say, "This is the amount I charge." Because when it's uncomfortable to ask for money and you are mixing it in with your self-worth, the judgements you have about yourself can prevent you from moving forward.

> ### EXERCISE: PAST EXPERIENCES OF ASKING FOR MONEY
>
> What are your past experiences with asking for money? Include:
>
> Pocket money
> Banks
> Mortgages
> Your partner
>
> Identify any negative experience in asking for money in your past and tap on it to release any emotion and transform the beliefs.
>
> **Example:**
>
> As a child, my client 'Jennifer' wanted to ask for some money for a school trip. She was about to go

> downstairs when she heard her parents arguing
> over the lack of money. She sat on the stairs and
> decided that she couldn't ask. She developed the
> beliefs in that moment that she was being selfish by
> asking for money and that there wasn't enough to
> go around.

Our rates need to reflect the value of the service we're
giving. If we underprice it, our prospective clients devalue
it in their minds too. So, valuing yourself ripples out to your
clients and to everyone that you reach with your services.

> **REFLECTION POINT:**
>
> When people ask you how much you charge, do
> you feel congruent with the amount or are you
> nervous when you tell them your rate?

When you're limiting yourself to how much you believe
you can ask for and if you're not fully congruent with what
you are charging or what you are asking for, you send a
message out that you don't deserve what you desire.

Any incongruence or nervousness will be received by
your prospective client. If they feel that you are nervous,
unsure or not clear, it may affect their buying decision.

A great, simple exercise one of my clients did for her
'tapping' homework was to stand in front of a mirror each
day and repeat her amount: "My charges are £75.00 for a
one-hour session or £300 for five sessions," tapping on the
emotion that it brought up. She would also have her friends
ask her, "What are your charges?" and would practice.
Within ten days she was speaking with a potential client

and it flowed beautifully. The client said, "Great ... and how do I make the payment for five sessions to you?"

EXERCISE: INCREASING YOUR RATES

Tune into the amount that you're currently charging. Begin tapping on your finger points. Check how comfortable you are with your current rates.

How comfortable would you feel asking for more? Is there a limit to how much you believe you can ask for? Tap if it feels uncomfortable to raise your rates (tip: it is probably going to or you would likely have raised them already!).

See, feel or hear the new amount. Then add another £10.00, $10.00 or 10 euros to that amount. Imagine that amount on your website. Hear yourself telling your clients how much you're charging and notice what that brings up in your body.

Tap on any uncomfortable emotions that this brings up (and use the Movie Technique or Matrix Reimprinting for any possible memories that need resolving).

Come back to that amount and once it feels comfortable, add another £10.00, $10.00 or 10 euros. Go through the same process until it is comfortable.

Keep going until you have doubled your current rates. Now, I'm not suggesting that you have to double your rates! But being emotionally and energetically open to receiving more will enable you to receive the money you desire (rather than being short on it). Expand the amount when you are ready to do so.

EFT Master and Matrix Reimprinting Creator Karl Dawson often shares this anecdote on his courses. A Reiki practitioner put an announcement in the newspaper, advertising sessions at £200. Somebody phoned to book an appointment with him and said, "OK, so your sessions are £200 — is that for an hour or an hour and a half, or is that two hours? How long is the session?" When the Reiki practitioner told the prospective client that there was a mistake and the sessions were actually £20, the prospective client made an excuse and didn't book. In her mind a £200 Reiki session was going to be better than a £20 one, even though it is the same universal energy!

You need to be aware of the value that people place on what they are getting. If you undercharge, you not only do yourself a disservice, but you do the same to your clients.

The Price(lessness) of Transforming Issues

Remember, your clients often save money by working with you! Have any of your clients ever shared with you how much money it's actually saved them when they stopped smoking, for example? If someone spent £500 and stopped smoking with you, how much would they save just on no longer needing to buy cigarettes (and we all know that in calculating the reduction of their future health risks, £500 would not come near the cost of treating some of the diseases that are related to smoking).

How much would it be worth to somebody to lose weight? How much would you be prepared to pay to have somebody assist you to lose that weight? It isn't just about losing weight. Someone might come to us with a weight issue, but we know that we help them with their self-esteem and the underlying emotional issues that are causing them to overeat. How much is that worth (again, not even calculating the future risks of heart disease, diabetes and so on)? This is the true value of what your sessions are worth. Suddenly wavering about whether you should charge £50 or £60 an hour seems like a drop in the ocean!

HOW LONG ARE YOUR SESSIONS?

Another part of charging what you are worth is ensuring that you have boundaries around your sessions. If you are advertising an hour for £60, then what is your system if you go over that time? It can help to ask your client before the session starts, "If we get into some deep emotional issues, I may ask you if you want to continue after the hour. Is that OK with you? I will always give you the choice either way." This prevents you from feeling like you have to 'fix' everything within the hour, and also lets your client know of your procedure, should you run over. This is where creating packages comes in useful, because you can 'borrow' time from a future session if you get into some challenging issues.

GUIDELINES ON CREATING PACKAGES

When clients come for more than one session, you can reward them for doing so by creating a package.

One of the advantages is that clients who commit to packages aren't expecting a one-hit wonder. It enables them to see that working with you is a process and you are offering a long-term solution rather than a quick fix.

Usually packages are paid for upfront. For example, if your rate is £60 an hour, then you might offer five sessions for the price of four at £240.

SKYPE OR TELEPHONE RATES

Sometimes people ask if they should reduce their rates when working over Skype or the telephone. I believe these modalities should be charged at the same rate because each has its own benefits. Both take up the same amount of time (although you probably won't need to rent out a space to carry them out, as long as you can work uninterrupted from home).

Skype and telephone sessions offer anonymity. I had a client from the US; she didn't want to give me her name because of the sensitive nature of her issues. Six months and twenty-five sessions later she revealed her name to me. It was only because I could offer her camera-free Skype sessions that we were able to reach this point.

One of my friends who has a very successful practice shared a funny story with me. She had a client who had experienced sessions with her for several months over Skype. Finally they got to work face-to-face. At the end of the session, he revealed that he preferred working with her on Skype. He said he found it much less distracting, felt much less self-conscious, and was much more focused as a result.

Your accessibility to people around the world is also something to consider and Skype and telephone sessions allow this. Be sure to tap on any blocks that you have to believing that Skype or telephone sessions are less valuable than face-to-face sessions.

Summary of Chapter Ten

a. **Money was born from an exchange system.** We sometimes forget that it is simply an exchange of energy.

b. **When we have judgements and conclusions about how we expect our relationship with money to be, we block our receiving.** Our energy contracts as a result, and we can't see or manifest solutions. A lot of the times we use money to limit our possibilities.

c. **If your money were your lover, what would you be saying to him or her?** Seeing your money as a lover will enable you to take a deeper look at your relationship with it and to transform that relationship.

d. **When you've got situations that occur over and over again with your money, such as getting into debt in familiar ways or going overdrawn and getting charged, it's usually because there's a comfort zone around the old pattern for you.** That comfort zone has been created from your belief systems. Emotionally and energetically, it is easier to stay with what we know financially than 'rocking the boat' and enabling change so that we can have all that we have dreamed of.

e. **When you think about asking for money, what happens in your body?** You need to ensure you are comfortable with asking for what you are worth.

f. **Your clients often save money by working with you!** When you help them resolve issues, it saves them time, money and energy in the long run.

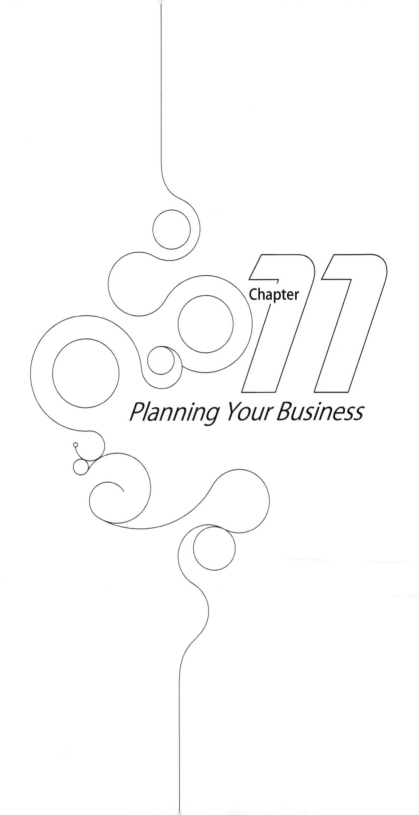

Chapter **11**

Planning Your Business

When it comes to business planning, you need to take a two-pronged approach.

On the one hand, if you don't plan at all, your business will be like a ship without a rudder. In addition, if you don't tell the universe what you are asking for, it will be trickier for you to manifest it.

On the other hand, if you overplan, you don't leave any room for innovation or expansion. The challenge is, particularly if you are doing a lot of work on yourself, you are not going to be the same person in six months' time as you are today. If you make a rigid plan that doesn't allow for your growth, you can get caught up in it, not allowing yourself to expand into something greater.

Business planning is an art, and not one that is learnt overnight. There needs to be a balance between your structure and your flexibility. In this chapter, we will begin to lay out a plan for you, and we will continue in the chapter that follows, in which I will share a number of exercises and techniques that will enable you to support that plan on an energetic level.

YOUR RELATIONSHIP TO PLANNING

We'll start with your relationship to planning, because it often brings up a lot of tappable tension for many of us. If you grew up in the West, unless you went to a very progressive school (such as a Steiner School), chances are that your timetable was planned in a way that felt restrictive to you. The Western education system herds us from one lesson to the next, and we learn to conform to (or rebel against) a system that many of us 'free thinkers' find restricting. This has left us with a challenging relationship with planning. I personally had pretty much every second of my life planned out as a child with school, dance lessons and competitions. There was very little breathing room to be me. And as a result, when I became an adult, I rebelled, and felt resentful whenever I had to plan. However, there was still a big part of me that had that drive to plan. It was the kind of drive that led me to burn myself out with chronic fatigue. There was a conflict within me between the rebel and the one that wanted everything controlled and ordered and just so.

I've found that many of my clients have been able to relate to this in some way. There is a part of us that wants to be free, unstructured and able to choose and create life from moment to moment. There is a part of us that wants to create a structure and a plan. When we get both these parts in balance we can plan *and* leave space for our creativity and for new things to come in. If either part gets out of balance, it can mean either the sergeant major or the 1960s love child is in charge! And as I am assuming you wouldn't put either of these two in charge of your business, it is vital that your planning come from a place where the two energies are working together. Otherwise you will have times when you are just pushing yourself all the time and others when you are completely opting out.

EXERCISE: YOUR RELATIONSHIP WITH PLANNING

Close your eyes and begin tapping. Bring before you your different planning styles as characters. If you are an efficient planner, there may be only one. If you are an erratic planner, there may be several.

Notice the positive qualities of each and thank them each in turn for their contribution. Also note the more destructive styles of each. Tap to bring down any negative emotions that may be associated with their more destructive behaviours. You may need to work with them one at a time in order to clear any negative emotions that are arising.

Now ask what needs to happen for them all to work together? Do they need to merge into one character with a higher intelligence incorporating all of their characteristics? Or do they need to maintain their individuality but learn new, more supportive ways of functioning?

When there is a healthy picture between you and them, borrow the reimprinting process from

> Matrix Reimprinting, taking the picture through the top of your head, allowing all the cells of the body to resonate with the new information, and then sending it out through your heart and into the universe.
>
> Repeat regularly until you have a healthier relationship with the planning aspect of yourself.

Once you have completed this exercise, you are ready to write your goals down.

Why Writing Down Your Goals is Important

When you think about a goal inside your mind, it is not something that is tangible. There may be energy behind it, but if you don't write it down, it can quickly dissipate. Action is always required to transform an initial idea into a reality. When you write your goal down, a chemical release occurs as you put pen to paper.

There are more and more studies substantiating that learning increases, as does the realisation of goals, through the physical act of writing things down.

A study by a professor at the Dominican University of California found that people who wrote their goals down and shared them with others were 33% more likely to achieve them versus those who did not write down their goals. (See http://www.dominican.edu/dominicannews/dominican-research-cited-in-forbes-article for more information.)

There are a number of powerful cells grouped together at the base of our brain; they work in conjunction with the

Law of Attraction. These cells form the Reticular Activating System or RAS for short. The RAS is responsible for sensing things around us and sorting them out for us. This system helps us in every part of our daily life. It is also responsible for filtering out what is important and so if you have focused your thoughts, this gives the RAS the heads up that it is important to you.

By the act of writing, you are focusing your thoughts, increasing your concentration and performing a physical action with your hand. You are focusing on the words, and time is taken to connect with them. Many parts of your brain are being activated at the same time, including the RAS, which then deems what you have written to be important. This could be why writing has more potency than typing for a number of people.

The science behind why is explained by author Henriette Anne Klauser in her book *Write It Down, Make It Happen*. She states that "Writing triggers the RAS, which in turn sends a signal to the cerebral cortex: Wake Up! Pay attention! Don't miss a detail! Once you write down a goal, your brain will be working overtime to see you get it, and alert you to all the signs and signals that were there all along."

There are also studies that show that writing aids the long-term memory. This could explain why we can write down a goal and years later achieve it, although we may have thought that we had forgotten all about it. The RAS had been working on it all along!

The RAS goes into overdrive when connected with visualisation, dreams and goals. It will programme itself to look for the possibilities and opportunities to make them happen.

So if you have a goal or dream you wish to realise, then write it down. Supercharge those cells and they will, in turn, work on achieving it for you.

Breaking Down Your Goals into Manageable Steps

When it comes to writing down your goals, you need to do so in a way that feels manageable to you. If you hear the word 'business plan', it might trigger some issues for you. But business planning is really just breaking your goals down into manageable steps.

Instead of trying to create a formal business plan, simply start with the broader question of what it is you would like to create in your business. For example, "By the end of the year I will be working consistently with twelve clients a week in a therapy centre." (Notice how I framed this as though it is going to happen. Always use "I will be" instead of "I would like to be.")

Now jot down all the things that need to happen in order for you to create that. Remember, if you get overwhelmed, you are in a far better position than most people who carry out an exercise such as this—tapping can change the way you feel about it almost instantly!

Now, what five initial steps can you take to help you accomplish your goals for your EFT business?

Dedicate time in your diary to complete these steps.

Remember <u>Not</u> to Plan Each Tiny Step

So, the worst thing you can do right now is try and plan every single step you need to achieve in order to reach your goal. Aside from overwhelming yourself, if you do this, you will suffocate your project. You will be so busy focusing on the minor details of how you think it should be that you will end up missing the neon signs that the universe is giving you. (In Chapter 12 we will explore this further when we look at manifesting your business.)

Creating a Wider Plan

As well as the smaller steps, look at some of the broader steps you can take to bring clients into your business.

Ask yourself the following questions:

"What can I do on a weekly basis to connect with potential clients?"

"What can I initiate once a month to gain a bigger presence?" (such as presentations, talks, radio interviews, magazine articles, blogs, and so on)

"What can I do once or twice a year to entice my clients?" (such as events or special offers)

By creating ahead of time the goals to do something weekly, something monthly and something once or twice a year, you are starting to look at the bigger picture of your business. Ensure you have a way of recording and monitoring the bigger picture interventions, so they don't just become ideas that you fail to follow through on.

When you have your shorter-term and longer-term goals, you can write these out into one plan for the whole year. Often, booking a one-off session with a business planner who knows your industry can be a great way to commit your plan to paper.

Financial Planning Exercise

It is helpful to do some financial planning as part of your overall planning. Financial planning is working out the (realistic) amount you would like to generate in your business in the next year. In order to plan financially, you always need to make sure you are in alignment with that which you are asking for.

FINANCIAL PLANNING EXERCISE:
PART ONE: WHAT DO YOU WANT?

Start by writing down the number of hours you have available for clients, teleseminars, webinars, workshops, and so on.

Now answer the following questions:

- What would you like your business to be financially providing for you?
- What lifestyle would you like your business to be providing for you?
- What would you like to be experiencing or having in this lifetime?
- What are the benefits to your life that your business could be bringing in? (new car, holidays, etc.)

Ask yourself if you are going to be able to achieve those goals on your projected income. Look at the lifestyle that you want and then ask yourself if the business is going to be able to provide it for you.

Take your time answering the questions in Part One. These are not questions that can be answered in a few minutes. Really connect with yourself and your desires. Then, and only when you have completed Part One, move forward to Part Two below. Again take your time with Part Two and then you will be ready to undertake the emotional clearing in Part Three.

FINANCIAL PLANNING EXERCISE:
PART TWO: THE MATHS!

1. Write a list of all monthly outgoings, including all annual bills, payments and taxes.
2. Write down all your monthly living expenses, e.g. food, coffee, household shopping.
3. Then add in figures for additional outgoings that you choose such as holidays, exercise classes.
4. Include personal/business development courses, birthday presents, evenings out, clothing, reading, etc.
5. Add in any debts or other regular payments you have to make.
6. Add in any savings that you want to be making, including pension pot and emergency savings pot.
7. Do you have a pot just to have fun with? If not, add in 10% of the total so far. This account is just for you to treat yourself with, so that you have those new shoes, new golf clubs, weekends away. This 10% is for pure spending pleasure each month.
8. Total your monthly figure.
9. Then look at how many hours are available and see how you will most likely use the time available for work to its maximum. For example, if you have six client hours per week but want £5,000 per month, this revenue isn't necessarily going to come from clients alone. Instead you could work with three clients and deliver webinars, evening

groups and workshops to help you have different income streams. This can help you figure out the possibilities that are available to you outside of one-to-one sessions.

FINANCIAL PLANNING EXERCISE: PART THREE: THE EMOTIONS

Now that you have the new monthly figure, how does it make you feel—lighter or heavier? Be aware of your mind chatter once you have completed the exercise. This is where the resistance will come in.

This figure is what you really need to live per month and have quality of life. This is a need rather than a luxury.

Do you deserve this life? Is this a life you are ready, willing and able to step into? A life where you have everything you desire? A life where there is no worry about money? Where you have complete possibility and opportunity? A life of financial freedom? Tap on any resistance.

Do your current earnings from your EFT practice give you this lifestyle now? I'm suspecting that the answer might be no (or else you wouldn't have bought the book!).

Ask these questions individually:
"Where am I blocking me?"
"Why am I blocking me?"
"How am I blocking me?"
"When am I blocking me?"
"What benefit do I get out of not receiving the life I desire to live?"
"What's the value of stopping myself from achieving this life?"

> Tap on anything and everything that comes up in each individual question.

Clearing your blocks to receiving will mean that you will be able to make a plan for your business that you can continually grow and evolve. The key is to keep planning and tap on any blocks you have to achieving your dreams. It is an ever-evolving and dynamic process that requires your consistent participation.

Summary of Chapter Eleven

a. **If you don't plan at all, your business will be like a ship without a rudder.** In addition, if you don't tell the universe what you are asking for, it will be trickier for you to manifest it.

b. **If you overplan, you don't leave any room for innovation or expansion.** Overplanning means smothering your project.

c. **Business planning is an art, and not one that is learnt overnight.** There needs to be a balance between your structure and your flexibility.

d. **Check your relationship to planning.** Create a balance between your organiser and your free spirit.

e. **Write down your goals.** It stimulates the Reticular Activating System (RAS), which is responsible for sensing things around us and sorting them out for us. By the act of writing, you are focusing your thoughts, increasing your concentration and performing a physical action with your hand, all of which bring the RAS into action.

f. **There are studies that show that writing aids the long-term memory.** This could explain why we can write down a goal and years later achieve it, although we may have thought that we had forgotten all about it. The RAS had been working on it all along!

g. **When it comes to writing down your goals, you need to do so in a way that feels manageable to you.** Instead of trying to create a formal business plan, simply start with the broader question of what it is you would like to create in your business. Then jot down all the things that need to happen in order for you to create that.

h. **As well as the smaller steps, look at some of the bigger steps you can take to bring clients into your business.** Look at this in terms of the next weeks, months and years.

i. **It is helpful to do some financial planning as part of your overall planning.** Financial planning is working out the (realistic) amount you would like to generate in your business in the next year.

Chapter

12

Manifesting Your Business

What's the one advantage you have as an EFT practitioner over those who practice other modalities when it comes to manifestation?

It's not a trick question! You have a tool, literally at your fingertips, that can enable you to clear the blocks that are preventing you from manifesting the business of your dreams. However, as you are probably already aware by now, tapping is not just for clearing your issues. It can be used to reinforce your goals too.

EFT Master Karl Dawson (who created the popular tapping technique Matrix Reimprinting) shares his theory about how tapping can be used in this way. Matrix Reimprinting is much about the 'pictures' that we hold in our energy fields from what went before. Matrix Reimprinting is different to the Movie Technique, which takes the energetic charge out of a picture. Instead, Matrix Reimprinting allows us to change the pictures that we hold. According to Karl, the new positive pictures that we create hold a much higher resonance than the old negative ones, and they allow our subconscious to tune into a different story about ourselves than the one that actually occurred.

Much of this book has been about clearing the old story around your business so that you can create a new one. Whether you have been using regular EFT or Matrix Reimprinting, now that you have cleared away some of the rubble of the past, you can start to reinforce your changes by creating new, positive pictures. The more you do this, the more you will resonate with the higher frequencies of your business. Your old doubts and worries will lose their power, because they will be replaced by a new, optimistic energy.

Remember, as well as planning your business, we want to enable you (as they say in Access Consciousness) to live in the question. Living in the question is constantly being open to something new happening.

Meditation teacher Sandy Newbigging (author of *Mind Calm*) once shared a story that highlights what it is like to live in the question. For some time he was raising a little girl. When she was about three years old, she would walk into the room full of excitement and anticipation. With eyes wide, she would draw in a breath and ask, "What's going to happen?" in the most joyful and innocent way. Now I want to ask you a question. What if you operated your business from this childlike energy? What if you operated from pure possibility and potential, constantly with eyes wide about who was going to walk through the door and what kind of connections you were going to make? If you practice the exercises in this chapter regularly (alongside clearing anything from the past that is in your way), you will be able to do just that.

Magnet Exercise

This first exercise is going to enable you to draw that which you want to manifest towards you. It is adapted from *Creating Money: Attracting Abundance Book* by Sanaya Roman and Duane Packer.

EXERCISE:

Bring your attention into your heart. Close your eyes and begin gently tapping.

Breathe in and out a colour that represents abundance.

Focus on a picture that represents you having the money you desire. What is it you see in that picture? Does it make you feel good?

Step into the picture, become the picture, feel the feelings, hear the sounds, touch the objects or the people involved.

Turn everything up: make the sounds louder, the objects more real, the feelings more powerful.

Just in front of your solar plexus, imagine a magnet coil or something that represents a magnet to you. See or feel that magnet growing and how it is drawing all those feelings and emotions to it.

Imagine everything that needs to happen to make this picture. You can imagine the magnet drawing them to you. You don't need to consciously know what those things are, just be open and receive them.

Ask how many times you need to repeat this exercise for this to become a reality. Whatever number drops into your mind, just make a note to remember it and stay in the feeling: enjoy it and allow it to expand until it either dissipates or you feel it's complete. Then open your eyes.

Remember to repeat the magnet exercise as many times as is needed. It will enable you to change your resonance and attract more opportunities to you. Always clear any blocks that it brings up about receiving.

Future Self Exercise

The following exercise was developed by Andrea Pusey. It will enable you to tune into a future version of yourself and reinforce the positive image of a future, more successful you in your mind and energy field.

FUTURE SELF EXERCISE:

Close your eyes and start tapping.

Imagine a future version of yourself who has already reached the business goals that you desire. Look at the picture and observe what you see.

Step into the picture and connect with your future self. Does that future self know who you are?

Ask your future self for forgiveness. (This is essential to healing the parts of us which believe that we have given ourselves a hard time for not having done it sooner, not having been brave enough, etc.)

Ask your future self to tap on you if there is any emotion coming up for you. This is your time to ask them anything you want to. You may choose to ask them to tell you what needs to happen so that you can be where they are now. Is there anything you need to change or do in order to be them?

If there were any advice they could give you, what would it be? Be sure to take it on board.

Ask your future self to step inside of you so you can feel what it feels like to be them. Feel your body and your cells change as they do this. It is important to give this plenty of time to integrate. Feel the emotion and the change in energy. Allow the integration. If there is a problem with gaining full integration, then have your future self step outside of you and ask them why. It may be you need further tapping, haven't asked the relevant question or that this needs to be done at a later date.

> If you have completed the integration, ask your future self if they will stay inside you with all the consciousness of how they achieved this success.
>
> Allow yourself to complete the integration fully before opening your eyes. It is really important to just sit for 5-10 minutes after this exercise, drinking a glass of water.
>
> This exercise can change the energy over about a 2-3 week period (based on client experiences). It is important not to repeat this exercise too often as you are changing your energy by the integration. However, it can be great to add the next exercise as a follow-up.

FIELD CLEARING TECHNIQUE

This exercise was created by Sasha Allenby (co-author of *Matrix Reimprinting Using EFT*). Although it was originally intended for clearing fields of habit such as addictions, Sasha also adapted it for use in business.

The principle is that you repeat it every day for at least twenty-one days (the time it is said to take to forge new neural connections). Sasha also tells me that doing this exercise for twenty-one days in a row is what led her and Karl Dawson to securing a contract with Hay House for the Matrix Reimprinting book. She told me that she still practices this exercise regularly, particularly at the start of a new business venture, and believes that it has played a vital role in the success of her business over the years.

I love this exercise for its simplicity in bringing our logical minds, consciousness, energy and emotions into alignment. It gives us an opportunity to create action that is in direct alignment with our goals.

One of the keys to this exercise is the set-up statement.

To build it, you need to:

• Use present tense
• Keep it in the positive
• Keep it brief and specific
• Include an action word ending with '-ing'
• Include at least one dynamic feeling word or emotion word that resonates
• Create it specifically for your circumstances.

Including all these elements in your set-up statement really supercharges your technique.

Examples: I am loving the joy I feel as I work with ten clients each week.

I am happy and confident talking to the twenty people attending my workshop.

EXERCISE: FIELD CLEARING TECHNIQUE

Create your set-up phrase, based on what it is you would like to manifest. The more specific you are, the better. Choose or adapt one from the sample below or create your own. Use the same set-up statement for 21 days.

- 10 clients a week
- 20 participants on my workshop
- 50 attendees at my EFT talk
- 100 people on my free webinar
- 500 people on my mailing list
- Your ideas?

Create the set-up phrase from this statement. For example:

"Even though I haven't always had 14 clients a week, I deeply love and accept myself." (We will use the example of 14 clients per week throughout this sample, but you can obviously swap in your goal.)

Say the set-up phrase while tapping on the karate chop point: "Even though I haven't always _____ (what you are attracting), I deeply love and accept myself." (Repeat three times.)

Keep your eyes closed for the remainder of the technique (if this is comfortable for you). Tap using the following sequence:
• Tap on the top of your head as you say: "I haven't always_____" (what you are attracting). (For example: I haven't always had 14 clients per week.)
• Tap on the eyebrow as you say: "I want to always _____" (what you are attracting). (For example: I want to always have 14 clients a week.)
• Tap on the side of the eye as you say: "I choose to always _____" (what you are attracting). (For example: I choose to always have 14 clients each week).
• Tap under the eye as you say: "I love to always _____ (what you are attracting), because ..." and then list all the reasons why you want to have what you are asking for, either in your mind or out loud. Make sure you are feeling the love! (For

example: I love to always have 14 clients a week because it means I am living my purpose, doing the work I love and serving people.)

• Tap under the nose. As you do, ask yourself what your life looks like, now you are attracting what you have asked for. Either verbalise or bring to mind all the positive images you associate with it as though they are real in the present tense. (For example: seeing clients come through your door, a full diary, you going to workshops, smiles on your clients' faces, positive reviews and feedback: anything that makes you feel good.)

• Tap on the chin. As you do, ask yourself what you are hearing now that you are attracting what you want. What can you hear others saying about you? And what are you saying about yourself? You can say these out loud if it helps you to resonate with them more. (For example: Thanks for a great session. I'm living my purpose. I was born for this. My life is really changing from working with you.)

• Tap on the collarbone. Ask yourself what actions you need to take in order to manifest your goal. Either verbalise the actions, or just bring them to mind. Include things you need to do today, this week, this month, in 3 months and in the next year. If anything new comes to mind, make sure you make a note of it after the session.

• Tap under the arm. Ask yourself how you feel now you are attracting what you want. Picture your future self who has already achieved these goals and tune into how they feel. Allow the feeling of already achieving the goals to run through your body.

• Tap on the liver points (under the breast). Bring to mind all the successes you have already had in achieving this goal. These include your training courses, your life experiences and anything else you have done or learnt that has brought you to this point today. This is a chance to celebrate you and honour how far you have come, so take your

time here and focus on as many achievements you can think of that have brought you to this moment.
• Tap across the wrist. Remind yourself that you are a spiritual being in a human body. Allow all the patterns from this lifetime that have meant that you have forgotten this to dissolve. Remember yourself beyond your patterns and programmes. Allow anything that is in the way of this knowing to dissolve.
• Tap on the thumb. As you do, choose one image that you associate with what you are manifesting. Be sure that you are in the image and take this image into your mind. (You can choose one of the images from earlier, such as the smiles on your clients' faces. You can choose a different image every day.)
• Tap on the first finger. As you do, with the image in your mind, picture all the neurons in your brain reconnecting to make this image your reality.
• Tap on the middle finger. As you do, send a signal to every cell in your body that this is your new reality.
• Tap on your third finger. As you do, take the new image into your heart. Connect your heart, your brain, your solar plexus and your gut with the new image so that the whole of your core is resonating with it.
• Tap on your little finger. Send the new information into the field of energy around your body. As it arrives in your body field, allow it to connect with all the future people that you are going to help with this goal.
• Tap on the nine gamut point. As you do, send the new image out into the universe through your heart. Spend a minute or two doing this so there is a very strong sense of the new image out there.
• Tap on the karate chop point. As you do, bring to mind all the things you are grateful for in relation to achieving your goals. You can list these silently

> or out loud. List things from your past, present and
> future that you are grateful for.
> • Finish with a dance of gratitude, either in your
> mind or in reality, in order to seal the new belief
> with positive emotions!

Ensure you repeat the Field Clearing Technique every day for twenty-one days. It will totally change your relationship to whatever it is you are manifesting in business and in life.

Summary of Chapter Twelve

a. **Creating new positive pictures is a key part of business manifestation.** The positive pictures that we create hold a much higher resonance than the old negative ones, and they allow our subconscious to tune into a different story about ourselves than the one that actually occurred.

b. **If you live in the question with your business, you will be constantly open to something new happening.** This kind of open questioning invites new possibilities.

c. **The Magnet Exercise enables you to draw towards you the things that you desire in business and in life.**

d. **The Future Self Exercise enables you to energetically align with the part of yourself that has already achieved the goals you desire.**

e. **The Field Clearing Technique helps to rewrite your old patterns around business in both your brain and in the universe.** It is best practiced for twenty-one days for maximum results.

Conclusion

You hold in your hands the key to achieving a thriving practice. One where your purpose unites with your joy for life and you treat your own wellbeing with the same respect and reverence as you do that of your clients. It's a business that you are proud to put your name to. You deserve it, and being an autonomous, self-directed business leader is one of the things that you came here to do.

I don't need to remind you that this is a journey. Part of us wants to show up with everything neatly packaged and ready-made. But the truth is, we grow from ironing out the bumps and learning how to apply what it takes in order to succeed. Your business growth and your personal growth are one and the same — not two separate things. And while you tend to the garden of the things that have been holding you back, you can expand more and more into what you have set out to do, be or achieve.

In this book I have shared with you a three-pronged approach. The first is to clear the rubble of your programming so that you are no longer filtering the world through that which you have been taught. The second is to create new and positive relationships with your business through changing the pictures of the way you relate to it. The third is to take action in the real world.

I can't stress the importance of the third component enough. If I had one 'beef' with some of the major teachings of this industry, it would be this one: if we clear the energy of the past, then we will magically manifest the life that we want. In my experience, if we clear the energy of the past *and* take action in the real world, we will then manifest the life of our dreams.

Now that you have come to end of this book, ensure that you don't wait for the perfect moment to start taking action in your external reality. Don't become one of those EFT practitioners that taps and taps but doesn't take action. Don't hide behind EFT. If you wait for the perfect moment, you will be waiting forever. Throw yourself into your practice (provided you are qualified and in a reasonable place emotionally). Learn, make mistakes, grow and improve, all the time balancing your clearing with your manifesting and with your action in the real world. See yourself as a detective, constantly uncovering that which has been holding you back, and fearlessly moving beyond it.

I know where you are now. I've been there myself. Everything that I have shared with you in this book has come from my very raw and real experience of being out there with my skin off, having to look deeply at that which was holding me back so I could move beyond it. It wasn't a straightforward journey. There were many bumps and setbacks along the way. Even now when I set a new goal I have the same level of discomfort to go through before I step into it. But the techniques work and my own life is testament to that.

I wrote this book to inspire and empower you as you proceed on your personal journey of actualising your business. You have amazing talents and skills that will benefit the world, and hopefully you have felt supported and guided as you have worked through the steps in this book. I wish you every success as you dive deeply into creating the EFT practice of your dreams.

Resources

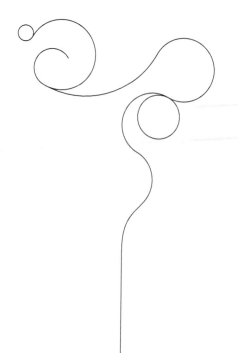

To learn Matrix Reimprinting or find a practitioner in your area, visit www.matrixreimprinting.com. You can also join the Facebook group: Matrix Reimprinting Using EFT.

Please choose www.YourEFTBusiness.com for:

- The link to the membership site for *Your EFT Business: The Essential Guide to Creating Your Dream Practice*. There, you'll find even more empowering practical business and emotional support
- Dedicated webinar programmes empowering EFT practitioners to realise their business dreams
- One-to-one business coaching sessions with Susie.

Bibliography

Arntz, William, and Chasse, Betsy, *What the Bleep Do We Know?: Discovering the Endless Possibilities for Altering Your Everyday Reality*, Health Communications, Deerfield Beach, Florida, USA, 2007

Byrne, Rhonda, *The Secret*, Atria Books, Hillsboro, Oregon, USA, 2006

Canfield, Jack, *How to Get from Where You Are to Where You Want to Be: The 25 Principles of Success*, Harper Element, London, UK, 2007

Canfield, Jack, and Bruner, Pamela, *Tapping into Ultimate Success: How to Overcome Any Obstacle and Skyrocket Your Results*, Hay House UK, London, UK, 2012

Canfield, Jack, Hansen, Mark Victor, and Hewitt, Les, *The Power of Focus: How to Hit Your Personal and Financial Targets with Absolute Certainty*, Vermillion, London, UK, 2001

Coelho, Paulo, *The Alchemist: A Fable About Following Your Dream*, HarperCollins Publishers, London, UK, 2012

Dawson, Karl, and Allenby, Sasha, *Matrix Reprinting Using EFT: Rewrite Your Past, Transform Your Future*, Hay House, London, UK, 2010

Dawson, Karl, and Marillat, Kate, *Transform Your Beliefs, Transform Your Life, EFT Tapping using Matrix Reimprinting*, Hay House, London, UK, 2014

Ferriss, Timothy, *The 4-Hour Work Week: Escape the 9-5, Live Anywhere and Join the New Rich*, Crown Publishers, New York City, New York, USA, 2007

Hamilton, David R., PhD, *Is Your Life Mapped Out?: Unravelling the Mystery of Destiny vs Free Will* , Hay House, London, UK, 2012

Hamilton, David R., PhD, *Why Kindness is Good for You*, Hay House, London, UK, 2010

Hendricks, Gay, *The Big Leap: Conquer Your Hidden Fear and Take Life to the Next Level*, HarperCollins Publishers Inc, New York City, New York, USA, 2010

Hicks, Esther and Jerry, *Money and the Law Of Attraction: Learning To Attract Wealth, Health And Happiness*, Hay House Inc, Carlsbad, California, USA, 2008

Hill, Napoleon, *Think and Grow Rich*, Wilder Publications, Radford, Virginia, USA, 2007

Klauser, Henriette Anne, *Write It Down, Make It Happen: Knowing What You Want – And Getting It!*, Touchstone Books, New York City, New York, USA, 2001

Kiyosaki, Robert T., *Rich Dad Poor Dad: What the Rich Teach Their Kids About Money That the Poor and Middle Class Do Not!*, TechPress, Scottsdale, Arizona, USA, 1998

Lipton, Bruce H., *The Biology of Belief: Unleashing the Power of Consciousness, Matter and Miracles*, Cygnus Books, Santa Rosa, California, USA, 2005

Lipton, Bruce H., *The Honeymoon Effect: The Science of Creating Heaven on Earth*, Hay House UK, London, UK, 2013

Look, Carol, *Attracting Abundance with EFT*: *Emotional Freedom Techniques*, AuthorHouse, Bloomington, Indiana, USA, 2005

McTaggart, Lynne, *The Field: The Quest for the Secret Force of the Universe*, HarperCollins Publishers, London, UK, 2001

Ortner, Nick, *The Tapping Solution: A Revolutionary System for Stress-Free Living*, Hay House, London, UK, 2013

Pert, Candace, *Molecules of Emotion: Why You Feel The Way You Feel*, Touchstone, New York City, New York, USA, 1999

Presely-Turner, Louise, *Finding A Future That Fits: Achieve Your Dreams & Discover Your True Self*, Hay House UK, London, UK, 2012

Roman, Sanaya, and Packer, Duane, *Creating Money: Attracting Abundance*, H J Kramer/New World Publishing, Novato, California, USA, 2008

Williams, Robert M, *PSYCH-K... The Missing Piece/Peace In Your Life*, Myrddin Publications, Crestone, Colorado, USA, 2013

Acknowledgements

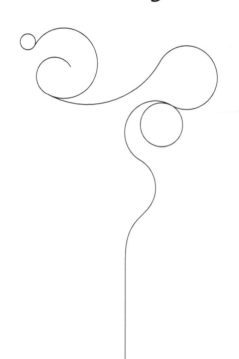

Karl Dawson: With the deepest of gratitude I would like to thank Karl Dawson. In September 2006, who knew as I sat sobbing in your garden therapy room what changes would be brought to my life? You inspired me and believed in me. Through your skill, knowledge, friendship and support you empowered me to turn around my health and my life. You inspired opportunity and possibility to grow in knowledge, belief and self. I am truly honoured to have been mentored by you and, more importantly, I am honoured to call you my friend.

Sasha Allenby: My friend, my confidante, my angel. Without you and your support, guidance and talent, there is no way this book would have come into existence. Throughout the years, you have challenged me, inspired me and helped me to step into the life I really wanted. We have laughed and cried together and you have always been there, encouraging me. Thank you my Angel Allenby.... We did good, girl!!!

To all my clients and course participants: Thank you for the opportunity to share these tools with you, to be a part of your journey and to be inspired by you.

Vera Malbaski: Thank you for the fabulous job you did with the transcriptions of my live webinar programmes for the book.

Lois Rose: Editor Extraordinaire! Thank you for being you. For being the warm welcome that I needed as this dream became a reality.

Star Restaurant, Avsallar: A big thank you to Mustafa, Ercan, and Elçin for your friendship and endless cups of tea and coffee, and to Ahmet Bey for the amazing food that kept my energy levels up whilst writing this book.

Andrea Pusey: For a session that sparked my dreams into reality, got my brain thinking and gave me the first glimpse that this book was to be written.

To those who have inspired and supported me professionally, thank you for your time, love and friendship: Ted Wilmont, Penny Croal, Carey Mann, Brett Moran, Annabel Fisher, David Hamilton, Richard Flook, Mark Whitehouse, Rebekah Roberts, Frank Swain, and Christine Southey.

To those who made my dream of travelling worldwide with EFT and Matrix Reimprinting a reality: Thank you ... Caroline Dawson, Barbara Belger, Dawn Gillespie, Gail Ferguson, Rob Nelson, Sabina Silc, Alenka Tercic, and Joanne Sparrow.

To my mum and dad: You have always supported me and helped me to be the best I can be. You taught me to 'go for it' as well as other valuable lessons I will hold close to my heart. Thank you so much for your continued encouragement and belief in me.

Dorothy and Andy: My friends and probably my surrogate parents. Thank you for being the amazing people you are and supporting me. I am truly grateful and blessed to have you in my life.

Jane Shaw: You have taught me so much over the years. You are my life mentor, my friend, my family and my fairy. I am so grateful that you are in my life.

Sharon King: Thank you for your friendship. How we have grown on our paths together! Thank you for your non-judgement, your love, support and endless telephone conversations.

Hazel Harrington: Twenty years of friendship … twenty years of being blessed that you are in my life. Your friendship, love and support mean the world to me.

To all those who helped my transition in Turkey:
Evrim: you took me in and offered me friendship (and cake!). I will never forget your kindness and generosity.

Hüseyin: you are an amazing soul and I am grateful to call you my friend / my brother. Thank you for all you have done for me by just being there.

Ülkü, my teacher, my mentor, my friend: Thank you.

Taylan Gundeşlioğlu of LetsGoToTurkey: Thank you for helping me joyfully and easily make my dream of living by the beach a reality.

Alanya Watersports, Vali, Fatih, Mehmet, Yusuf, Mehmet and Bülent … thank you for your kindness.

About the Author

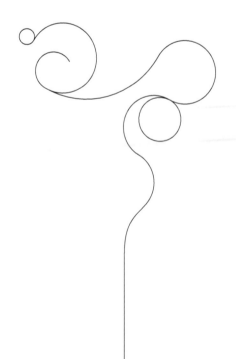

Susie Shelmerdine started her career in recruitment and conference organising and then set up her own company in the entertainment industry.

However, a chronic and disabling illness caused her to change track. After using EFT to heal herself, she became an internationally recognised EFT and Matrix Reimprinting practitioner and trainer, delivering courses in the UK, Europe, Australia, the US and Middle Asia.

Susie's excitement shines through when she is inspiring and empowering others to realise their dreams. She has helped EFT practitioners worldwide to become successful using the tools that she presents in this book. She is passionate about the ripple effect that is created when an EFT practitioner excels in their practice.

Susie has worked with owners of many types of businesses, with sales teams, sports personalities, entrepreneurs, property millionaires and banking organisations to help them increase their success and productivity — and to do so with heart.

Susie has used all the techniques that she shares in this book personally to transform her own life and realise her dreams. One of her dreams was to relocate to Turkey from the UK. She is now happily living there and regularly enjoys a swim with the turtles!

Printed in Great Britain
by Amazon